CAREERS IN THE US ARMED FORCES

CAREERS IN THE US MARINE CORPS

Taylor Baldwin Kiland and R. Conrad Stein

Enslow Publishing
101 W. 23rd Street
Suite 240
New York, NY 10011
USA

enslow.com

Published in 2016 by Enslow Publishing, LLC.
101 W. 23rd Street, Suite 240, New York, NY 10011

Library of Congress Cataloging-in-Publication Data

Kiland, Taylor Baldwin, 1966-
 Careers in the US Marine Corps / Taylor Baldwin Kiland and R. Conrad Stein.
   pages cm. — (Careers in the US Armed Forces)
 Includes bibliographical references and index.
 Summary: "Describes career opportunities in the US Marine Corps"—Provided by publisher.
 Audience: Grades 7-8.
 ISBN 978-0-7660-6947-3
 1. United States. Marine Corps—Vocational guidance—Juvenile literature. 2. United States. Marine
Corps—Juvenile literature. I. Stein, R. Conrad. II. Title.
 VE23.K54 2015
 359.9'602373—dc23
                                    2015015139

Printed in the United States of America

To Our Readers: We have done our best to make sure all Web sites in this book were active and appropriate when we went to press. However, the author and the publisher have no control over and assume no liability for the material available on those Web sites or on any Web sites they may link to. Any comments or suggestions can be sent by e-mail to customerservice@enslow.com.

Portions of this book originally appeared in the book *The Marine Corps and Military Careers*.

Photo Credits: Chip Somodevilla/Getty Images News/Getty Images, p. 7; Christine Yarusi, p. 1 (series logo); Colonel Charles Waterhouse, US Marines (Marine Corps Art Collection)/Wikimedia Commons/Attack on Derna by Charles Waterhouse 01.jpg/public domain, p. 15; Daniel Bendjy/E+/Getty Images, p. 1 (top right); DoD photo by Cpl. Pete Thibodeau, US Marine Corps., p. 4; DoD photo by Staff Sgt. D. Myles Cullen, US Air Force, p. 106; GERARD FOUET/AFP/Getty Images, p. 43; GrummelJS/Wikimedia Commons/Archibald Henderson.jpg/public domain, p. 58; GrummelJS/Wikimedia Commons/PresleyOBannon.jpg/public domain, p. 13; Ian Hitchcock/Getty Images News/Getty Images, p. 98; Marine Corps/Pfc. Alvin Pujols, p. 53; Mary Knox Merrill/The Christian Science Monitor via Getty Images, p. 64; MPI/Archive Photos/ Getty Images, pp. 31, 40; Paula Bronstein/Getty Images News/Getty Images, p. 45; Paul Thompson/FPG/ Getty Images, p. 20; PhotoQuest/Archive Photos/Getty Images, p. 29; Robert Nickelsberg/3rd Party - Misc/Getty Images, p. 85; Samuel Corum/Anadolu Agency/Getty Images, p. 59; Scott Olson/Getty Images News/Getty Images, pp. 67, 75; Stephen Morton/Photonica World/Getty Images, p. 70; Steve Cukrov/ Shutterstock.com (chapter openers); Stocktrek Images/Getty Images, pp. 83, 109; Straight 8 Photography/ Shutterstock.com, p. 1 (top left); US Air Force photo by Master Sgt. Adrian Cadiz, p. 50; US Marine Corps History Division, p. 18; US Marine Corps photo by Capt. Barry Morris, p. 71; ; US Marine Corps photo by Cpl. Joseph Scanlan, p. 80; US Marine Corps photo by Cpl. Laura Gauna, p. 97; US Marine Corps photo by Cpl. Michael C. Guinto, p. 93; US Marine Corps photo by Lance Cpl. Cuong Le, p. 110; US Marine Corps photo by Lance Cpl. Darien J. Bjorndal, p. 120; US Marine Corps photo by Lance Cpl. MaryAnn Hill, p. 69; US Marine Corps photo by Mass Communication Specialist 3rd Class Edward Guttierrez III, p. 105; US Marine Corps photo by Pfc. Alvin Pujols, p. 50; US Marine Corps photo by Pfc. Levi Schultz, p. 102; US Marine Corps Photo by Sgt. Anthony Kirby, p. 8; US Marine Corps photo by Sgt. Jennifer L. Jones, p. 90; US Marine Corps photo by Sgt. Marco Mancha, p. 56; US Marine Corps photo taken by LCpl. Aaron James B. Vinculado, p. 61; USMC photo 127-N-A2659/Wikimedia Commons/Marines on LVT at Inchon 1950. jpg/public domain, p. 37; US Navy photo by Photographers Mate 1st Class Ted Banks, p. 48; Wikimedia Commons/USMarine Corps Insignias/public domain, pp. 112, 113; W.wolny/Wikimedia Commons/3d Division Marines fan out.jpg/public domain, p. 24; W.wolny/Wikimedia Commons/Marines rest in the field on Guadalcanal.jpg/public domain, p. 26.

Cover Credit: Daniel Bendjy/E+/Getty Images (top right); Straight 8 Photography/Shutterstock.com (top left); Sgt. Alicia R. Leaders/US Marine Corps (bottom); Christine Yarusi (series logo).

frequently the "first in." In other words, they are some of the first uniformed Americans on the ground responding to the crisis. "Soldiers of the sea" is no longer an entirely proper name. Today's Marine units are frequently airlifted to their duty sites. Landlocked Afghanistan, for example, is nine hundred miles from the nearest seacoast.

Whether they travel by air or the sea, the Marine Corps has a long and proud history of serving the United States. Men and women of the United States Marine Corps (USMC) abide by an old message that sums up their spirit: "The Marines have landed; the situation is well at hand."

CHAPTER 2

THE FEW, THE PROUD

Resolved, That two battalions of marines be raised . . . that they be inlisted and commissioned to serve for and during the present war between Great Britain and the colonies . . .

—Excerpt from the Enabling Act, which gave birth to the Marine Corps on November 10, 1775[1]

It All Began in a Bar

In 1775, the United States was just beginning its war of independence against Great Britain. The Continental Congress (the predecessor to today's Congress) created the Marine Corps on November 10. One month later, at the Tun Tavern in Philadelphia, the first official Marine unit was formed, consisting of one hundred volunteers.

Officer William Eaton led a group of eight Marines and two Naval midshipmen more than 600 miles to capture the city of Derne during the First Barbary War.

Throughout the 1850s, the burning issue of slavery split the United States into two hostile camps. In October 1859, an antislavery zealot named John Brown took over a government arsenal at Harpers Ferry, Virginia. Brown and his small band of followers urged slaves to rise up in rebellion and join him at the arsenal. Once more, Marines were the first troops to arrive on the scene. A Marine unit broke into the firehouse the group had converted into a fort and captured John Brown. The Marines were led by Army Colonel Robert E. Lee, who later became the famous commander of the Southern forces. The Harpers Ferry raid was one of the events that fueled the start of the Civil War (1861–1865).

The Civil War divided the Marine Corps—much as the war divided the nation. About half of the men of the Corps resigned to fight with Confederate forces. Marines loyal to the Union served in sea battles at New Orleans and at Mobile Bay.

Fighting Fronts All Over the World

After the Civil War, many government leaders considered abolishing the, Marine Corps. They believed Army troops could readily take over Marine duties. Still others argued that sea soldiers working closely with the Navy were needed to fight the "small wars" that often broke out in far-off ports. Finally, the government decided to keep the Marine Corps, although at minimum strength.

So-called small wars in the late 1800s and early 1900s kept the Corps on fighting fronts all over the globe. Marine units landed more than a dozen times on the coast of China to put down rebellions that threatened American interests. Men of the Corps performed similar missions in Panama, Nicaragua, and Haiti. Minor conflicts in Latin countries were sometimes called "banana wars." Some modern historians have cited the banana-war period as an example of the United States bullying its neighbors in Latin America.

In the Spanish-American War (fought between April and August 1898), Marines again were the first to fight. Marines were the first Americans to land in Cuba and the first to storm the shores of the Philippines. Marines also occupied the former Spanish territories of Guam and Puerto Rico.

Men of the Marine Corps faced grave dangers in the small wars of the early 1900s. They flushed deadly snipers from unseen positions and fought pitched battles with rebels. The men worked under the broiling sun while suffering from tropical diseases such as malaria. Some rose to tasks beyond their duties. In 1915, Sergeant Dan Daly fought in Haiti. While under fire, he pulled a submerged machine gun from a mountain stream. Daly's actions earned him the Medal of Honor, the highest award given to a United States service member. It was Daly's second such honor. Sergeant Dan Daly remains the only Marine-enlisted man to ever receive two Medals of Honor. Smedley D. Butler, who served as a Marine officer in the banana-war period, also was given the nation's highest award twice.

Marines in World War I

In August 1914, World War I began in Europe. Military leaders believed the conflict would be short-lived. In its beginnings, the war appealed to European patriotism. Soldiers marched out of villages while bands played and neighbors cheered. No one imagined the battlefield effect of new weapons such as machine guns and fast-firing artillery. World War I ground down to static, ugly trench warfare. Huge armies fought each other from trenches separated by scarred ground often just a football field in length. In the mud of those long ditches, the pride of European youth bled and died.

The United States entered World War I in April 1917 when Congress declared war on Germany. Upon arriving at the battlegrounds, Marines and Army troops encountered the same grim trenches where Europeans had fought for years. Like the Europeans, the Americans lived in the muddy ditches along with rats and swarms of insects.

Amphibious warfare, the Marine specialty, was not employed by the Corps in World War I. Instead, the Marines were used as regular infantry. They often served under Army field officers. In combat, all American forces faced

Sergeant Major Dan Daly received the prestigious Medal of Honor twice, an extremely rare feat. The Medal of Honor is the US military's highest honor. It is given for personal acts of valor above and beyond the call of duty.

murderous artillery, poison gas, and deadly machine guns. In the summer of 1918, a fresh group of Marines occupied a trench line just in time to meet a German offensive. A French colonel suggested the Marines retreat rather than confront the advancing Germans. To this suggestion the Marine commander reportedly said, "Retreat, hell! We just got here."[2]

In June 1918, the Fourth Marine brigade repelled a German advance through a forest named Belleau Wood. During this storied battle, the young men discovered the mind-numbing horror of war. Veteran German machine gunners rained deadly fire on the Marines. In one day, the men of the Corps suffered eleven hundred killed or wounded.[3] This one-day figure at Belleau Wood was greater than the total number of casualties the Marines had endured in their entire previous history. Still the Marines triumphed, repelling the ongoing German assaults six times over the course of several weeks. German soldiers were so impressed with the fighting skills of these special American troops that they called them *Teufel Hunden,* German for Devil Dogs.

World War I ended with the armistice signed November 11, 1918. Though the war was a violent part of American history, two Marine firsts occurred during the war years. On August 13, 1918, Opha Mae Johnson became the first woman Marine. During World War I, several hundred women served in the Corps, performing mainly secretarial duties. Women service in the Marines was discontinued after World War I. In July 1918, the 1st Marine Aviation Air Force began operations in France. Marine pilots had trained in naval aviation schools earlier, but the World War I unit was the true beginning of Marine aviation.

US Marines were called to Europe to fight in World War I.

At first, the bloody clash of arms of World War I was called the Great War due to its vastness and the terrible number of people killed. It was also called the "war to end all wars" because it was generally thought humankind would never again be so foolish to enter a war of similar dimensions. But history soon wrote a sad message to those who believed the carnage of World War I would end all wars.

Marine Nicknames

Through the years the Marines have acquired several often-used nicknames:

Devil Dogs—The German name of respect given the Marines in World War I.

Gyrenes—The source of this term is obscure, but it was once used by British marines. The Corps picked up the nickname during the World War I years.

Jarheads—This term comes from a uniform that was used in the 19th century and had a collar so high it appeared the Marine's head was screwed into his neck.

Leathernecks—This originates with the leather collar Marines wore back in the 1800s. It is generally believed the leather collar uniform protected a man's neck during a sword fight.

CHAPTER 3

THE SECOND WORLD WAR

My heart pounded inside whenever I saw a buddy get hit and even more so when they died. We were taught to carry on and we knew we could not stop and dwell on the tragedy around us.

—Robert Jones, a Marine veteran of the Pacific War[1]

Two decades after the World War I armistice, the United States was forced back into a world war again after the Japanese made a surprise attack at Pearl Harbor on December 7, 1941. World War II was the coming-of-age for the Marine Corps and their battles were fought almost exclusively in the Pacific theater against the Japanese.

There, the Marines were in the forefront of an island campaign. Island battles called upon their special skills in waging ship-to-shore warfare. American strategists viewed the Pacific islands as stepping stones or as rungs of a ladder. Each island conquered served as an advanced base. Airfields and supply dumps were built on the islands. The conquest of every new island was a new step on the march to Japan.

No other branch of the armed forces was so well trained and well equipped for amphibious warfare as were the Marines. Beginning in the 1920s, General John Lejeune insisted the Corps return to its roots as soldiers of the sea. Just before World War II, General Howland Smith supervised training exercises that saw large Marine units assault beaches. Two new landing craft were developed during the practice maneuvers. The Higgins boat was a flat-bottomed craft that held twenty to thirty assault troops. Men climbed from ships onto Higgins boats, which then took them to an enemy beach. Another landing craft, the amphibious tractor, had tank-like treads and was able to climb up the hostile beach.

Furious combat took place on these Pacific islands. Japanese soldiers served under a code called *bushido*, or "way of the warrior." To them, death in battle was acceptable, even glorious. Surrender, on the other hand, was an unthinkable disgrace. For more than three years, Marines landed on the hostile shores of islands held by these fanatical defenders. With the sea at their backs, the Marines had no choice but to move forward against an enemy pledged to kill them or die in the attempt. Young men barely out of high school fought and died over specks of land they had never heard of before—

US Marines storm the shores of Bougainville Island during World War II. The Allied forces fought the Japanese for nearly two years for control of the island.

Guadalcanal, Tarawa, Kwajelein, Saipan, Tinian, Peleliu, Iwo Jima, Okinawa.

By 1944, more than 475,000 men and women were serving in the Marine Corps. The American public hailed the Marines as elite infantry troops who were given the toughest job of the war. Hollywood churned out movies celebrating Marine heroism. But those fighting in the Pacific found no glamour in the war. They saw island battlefields strewn with bodies, all bloated and rotting under the tropical sun. In the jungles of the South Pacific, thousands of Marines contracted malaria and other tropical diseases. The sights, smells, and terror of island fighting stayed locked in men's minds for years afterward.

The Battle of Guadalcanal

From the deck of a ship, this small island looked lush and green, ringed by a silvery white beach. It seemed to be everyone's idea of a Pacific paradise. Eleven thousand Leathernecks splashed ashore in August 1942. There, they discovered the hidden horrors of Guadalcanal—spiders the size of golf balls, nightmarish looking land crabs, beetles as big as a man's thumb, and ferocious white ants whose bite stung like a needle.

The Japanese were building an airstrip on Guadalcanal. To drive the Marines off the island, they launched furious counterattacks by sea, land, and air. Warships sailing off the beaches poured shell after shell on Marine positions. Enemy planes dropped bombs. On the rain-swept night of September 12, thousands of Japanese soldiers charged the Marines. The Americans fought back with machine guns, light artillery, rifles, bayonets, and even rocks and clubs. Marine lines held. But the morning after the battle, the island smelled of blood and death.

The Battles of Tarawa and Peleliu

No other invasion symbolized the deadly nature of World War II amphibious operations more than Tarawa. The tiny island of Betio, the main target of the Tarawa chain, is surrounded by a coral reef. Marines landed on the island in November 1943. Some of their landing craft were amphibious tractors, called amtracs. The amtracs crawled over the coral propelled by their tank-like treads. But many landing boats were Higgins boats and were not equipped with treads. Those on board the Higgins boats had to jump out and wade through a lagoon while enemy machine guns blazed away

Marines take a break from the fighting at the Battle of Guadalcanal, the first major offensive against the Japanese.

Sergeant Basilone Kept Firing

In a frantic Guadalcanal battle in October 1943, Sergeant John Basilone of Raritan, New Jersey, kept firing his machine gun even though he was surrounded by attacking Japanese. When the machine gun overheated and failed to fire, Basilone held the enemy back by shooting his pistol. For his actions, Basilone was awarded the Medal of Honor. He was also sent back to the United States to participate in parades and other events designed to promote the war effort. Basilone soon felt guilty about being at home while his friends remained in the Pacific, and he asked to return to the fighting fronts. His request was granted, and Sergeant Basilone was killed in 1945 when his Marine unit attacked Iwo Jima. A statue in his hometown honors his memory.

at them. The waters turned pink with their blood. A sailor looking at the invasion through binoculars wrote, "Those poor guys plodding in chest-high water and getting shot down. I tried not to look, but I couldn't turn away. The horror of it hypnotized me."[2]

The Battle of Tarawa lasted only seventy-six hours, but it constituted slaughter on an unimaginable scale.[3] Marine casualties totaled 1,027 killed and twice that number wounded.[4] Months later, movies of American dead floating like logs in the lagoon were played in theaters in the United States. It marked the first time in World War II that films showed large numbers of American dead. The movie showings were ordered by President Franklin Roosevelt.

The president wanted the public to realize the sacrifice of their armed forces. Many people left the movie houses in tears.

Peleliu was another island hell. The conquest of this island began in September 1944 and was expected to take several days. Instead, the fighting dragged on for weeks. Marine Corporal Eugene Sledge was a twenty year old who participated in the invasion. Sledge later wrote a powerful memoir called *With the Old Breed at Peleliu and Okinawa*. Though he was a brave and dedicated Marine, Sledge told of a moment on Peleliu when weeks and weeks of intense combat finally overwhelmed him:

> *I felt myself choking up ... I began sobbing. The harder I tried to stop the worse it got. My body shuddered and shook. Tears flowed out of my scratchy eyes. I was sickened and revolted to see healthy young men get hurt and killed day after day. I felt I couldn't take it anymore.*[5]

Navajo Leathernecks

The Navajo American Indian tribe has a storied legacy in World War II. Books and movies have been written about their unique contribution to the war effort. Throughout the Pacific War, the Japanese tried to intercept American radio messages so they could anticipate their enemy's moves. Americans radioed in code, but the Japanese were skilled code-breakers. To counter Japanese intercepts, the Marines used Navajo Indians to relay orders by radio. Navajo is a complicated language spoken by only a few dozen people outside the tribe. The Marines gathered about four hundred enlisted men of Navajo descent and let them convey messages. They were sometimes called "windtalkers." The Navajos

To counter Japanese interceptions of American code the Marines counted on Navajo "windtalkers," including (left to right) Corporal Oscar Ithma, Private First Class Jack Nez, and Private First Class Carl Gorman.

converted their ancient language to conform to military terms: *besh-lo* (ironfish) meant submarine and *chay-da-gahi* (tortoise) meant tank. Navajo words baffled the Japanese. No message intercepted was understood by the enemy as long as it was broadcast by these Navajo "Code Talkers."

The Battle of Iwo Jima

On February 19, 1945, a huge fleet of American warships surrounded the tiny treeless island of Iwo Jima. Battleships, cruisers, and destroyers opened up with their big guns. The island disappeared under a cloud of exploding shells. At 7:30 in the morning, scores of landing craft, each crowded with up to twenty Marines, churned toward Iwo Jima. At the beach, ramps opened and the Marines charged out. At first, Japanese defenders held their fire. Then, with terrifying sudden-ness, artillery shells and machine-gun bullets screamed at the Marines. Desperately the Americans inched forward, crawling on their bellies like snakes. In minutes, twisted bodies of dead men lay sprawled on the sand. Wounded men shrieked in agony.

The furious battle for Iwo Jima raged day and night. On the morning of the fifth day, the Marines fought their way up Mount Suribachi, the ancient volcano that dominated the island. At the peak of the mountain they found a pipe they could use as a staff and they raised an American flag. Men below cheered at the sight of the Stars and Stripes waving in the wind. Ships offshore blew their whistles. It was deter-mined the first flag was too small. So a runner was sent to fetch a larger flag, and five Marines and a Navy medic raised the new banner. Newspaperman Joe Rosenthal photographed

This iconic image symbolizes the taking of the island of Iwo Jima.

this second flag-raising. Rosenthal had no idea he had taken the most famous photo of World War II.

The Battle of Iwo Jima lasted thirty-four days. Final victory came at a staggering cost in American blood: twenty-six thousand casualties including six thousand eight hundred dead.[6] Survivors of the battle were left almost paralyzed from horror and sheer exhaustion. Some Marines went insane due to the intense combat pressure.

Okinawa

Okinawa was the final island, the last rung on the ladder stretching to Japan. On April 1, 1945, Marines and Army troops landed, all of them believing this would be a ghastly fight. To everyone's surprise, the Americans quickly conquered the northern two thirds of the island. Then the real fight took

The Iwo Jima Memorial

At the time of Iwo Jima, the United States had been at war for more than three years. The public was war-weary. Then the dramatic picture of Marines raising the flag on a bleak mountaintop thrilled the people and boosted their morale. The photo became a part of the American memory forever. On November 10, 1954, President Dwight Eisenhower dedicated the Marine Corps War Memorial in Washington, D.C. An inscription on the base of the monument repeats the words of Admiral Chester W. Nimitz, who said of the fighting men on Iwo Jima, "Uncommon Valor was a Common Virtue."

General Pedro A. del Valle Led on the Frontlines

Born in San Juan, Puerto Rico, Pedro del Valle graduated from the US Naval Academy and was commissioned a Marine Lieutenant in 1915. He became an artillery expert, but he often led infantry troops. On Okinawa, he commanded the 1st Marine Division. In this capacity, he lived on the frontlines with his men and faced the same dangers they faced. For his exceptional leadership on Okinawa, Lieutenant General del Valle was given the Distinguished Service Medal.

place in the south. Okinawa proved to be the bloodiest battle of the Pacific war. Marines and army troops served side-by-side, trying to blast the Japanese defenders out of their caves and bunkers. At sea, naval ships suffered repeated attacks from kamikazes, the dreaded Japanese suicide bombers.

No one on the bloody island of Okinawa was aware of a supersecret operation called the Manhattan Project. The men and women involved in the Manhattan Project were developing an atomic bomb. At the time, Japan was an exhausted and virtually defeated nation. Some American leaders doubted the wisdom of using this powerful bomb on an already beaten nation. But the awful bloodletting on Iwo Jima and Okinawa erased all doubts. If US forces had to invade the Japanese home islands, the casualties could have been terrible. Some estimated that more than a million

American and Japanese lives would be lost in such a planned invasion. So, on August 6, 1945, a B-29 bomber dropped a single atomic bomb on Hiroshima. Tens of thousands of Japanese were killed in less than a minute. Three days later, another such bomb fell on Nagasaki. On August 14, Japan surrendered to the United States and its allies. World War II, one of the most terrible wars in world history, was over.

The Marines suffered almost ninety-two thousand total casualties (killed and wounded) during World War II. This was a shockingly high number for the smallest branch of the major services. The Marines made up less than 5 percent of the Americans who fought in World War II, yet the Corps suffered 10 percent of the country's total casualties.[7] Unfortunately, this would not be the last action they would see in the twentieth century.

CHAPTER

4

THE CORPS AND THE CHANGING WORLD

Half my casualties were from [Vietnamese] guerrillas, and these were the nasty kind of casualties—the dirty war.

—General Lew Walt, who commanded Marine forces in Vietnam in the late 1960s[1]

The last half of the twentieth century was dominated by the Cold War, a fifty-year struggle between the Communist and capitalistic governments. It was called the "Cold War" because there was no large-scale fighting between the two enemies, but there were regional wars in Korea, Vietnam, and Afghanistan. The Cold War split the World War II alliance between the United States and the Soviet Union. These two countries were the only two world superpowers, and they had vastly different governments and economies.

35

Often the two sides provided support for countries friendly to their system. In Korea, the communist governments in the Soviet Union and China gave aid to the North while the United States assisted South Korea. Marines fought in all these post-World War II conflicts.

The Korean War

On the morning of June 25, 1950, artillery roared over the 38th Parallel, the dividing line between Communist-ruled North Korea and South Korea. When the firing lifted, Soviet-built T-34 tanks led thousands of North Korean infantrymen into an attack on their southern neighbors. The Korean War had begun.

American troops were rushed to South Korea to stem the Communist advance. At first the American-led forces were pushed backward on the Korean Peninsula. Bravely, they defended a tiny corner of the land called the Pusan Perimeter. On September 15, 1950, army General Douglas MacArthur ordered soldiers and Marines to land at the port city of Inchon, which was far behind the Pusan front. For Marines, Inchon would be the last major ship-to-shore invasion they would make while under fire. Battling tricky tides as well as the enemy, the Marines established a beachhead at Inchon and marched inland. General MacArthur later wrote, "The Marines and Navy have never shone more brightly than this morning."[2]

The Inchon landings shattered the North Korean resistance. In late 1950, American forces drove deep inside North Korea. Then, just before Christmas, bugles sounded over the North Korean hills. Responding to the bugle calls, thousands of Chinese soldiers charged the Americans. The Chinese

US Marines roll into Inchon, after which they drove deeper into the interior of North Korea.

army had intervened and launched a new and ugly chapter of the Korean War.

The sudden Chinese attack left men of the 1st Marine Division trapped near the Chosin Reservoir. Temperatures fell to 20 degrees below zero, and blinding snow pelted the Marines. In the face of blasting winds, the men began a 78-mile trek to the port city of Hungnam. Everyone walked over the frozen roads. Only the wounded and dead rode in trucks. One wounded Marine saw "Bodies strapped on the barrels of artillery, on the sides of trucks, across hoods, anywhere there was space. They were rigid. A wounded guy next to me froze to death the second night."[3]

For the next two-and-one-half years, Americans and their United Nations (UN) allies fought Communist troops in Korea. It became a war of hills, as battles were concentrated on dismal rises in the earth. Americans gave nicknames to these places—Pork Chop Hill, Old Baldy, Heartbreak Ridge.

As the Korean War continued, the American public coped with the frustrating situation by ignoring events in that far-flung land. News of the Korean War slipped from page one in the newspapers to page seven or eight. Some political leaders suggested Korea was a "police action," not a war. But Marines battling for the stark hills knew this looked like war, smelled like war, and hurt like war. A grim joke was told at the fighting fronts: "If this is a police action, why didn't they send cops?"

It would take more than three years of fighting before an armistice was signed on July 27, 1953, officially ending the conflict. By that time, more than thirty-three thousand Americans had died in the war.[4] The agreement created the

Korean Demilitarized Zone (DMZ) to separate North and South Korea.

In July 1995, President Bill Clinton dedicated the Korean War Veterans Memorial on the National Mall in Washington, D.C. Looming high off the ground are nineteen larger-than-life infantrymen who march cautiously toward an American flag. Their faces bear the haunting expressions of men at war—confused, frightened, lonely. The monument stands as a powerful reminder of this costly war.

The Vietnam War

No war since the Civil War divided the American public as did Vietnam. The Vietnam War began in the late 1950s when Communist North Vietnam clashed with the armies of South Vietnam. Many believed this was an Asian civil war that Americans should avoid. American presence began with small forces, but it soon escalated.

Once more, the Marines were first to fight. In March 1965, two battalions of Marines, about thirty-five hundred men, were sent to South Vietnam to protect the airbase at Da Nang. This was a dramatic change in US policy. Previously, only advisors and other special troops had served in Vietnam. The Marines were the first regular ground forces sent to the country. Those men of the Corps had no idea they were the start of a war that would last seven frustrating and bloody years.

By 1968, some eighty-five thousand Marines, a quarter of the Corps' strength, were serving in Vietnam.[5] The Marines fought major battles at Khe Sanh and in the Hai Lang Forest. The twenty-five-day battle for the city of Hue remains a bitter chapter in Marine history. Marines were reluctant to use artillery in Hue City because it was crowded with civilians. Blasting the houses with artillery shells would cause terrible civilian casualties. So the men patrolled the city with rifles and fought the North Vietnamese and Vietcong street by street and house by house. More than one thousand Marines were killed or wounded in the ordeal at Hue.[6]

Over the course of the war, which lasted from 1964 until 1975, a total of 14,844 Marines were killed in action, twenty-five percent of the 58,220 Americans who were killed in the war.

In 1982, the Vietnam Veterans Memorial was dedicated in Washington, D.C. The memorial consists of a black granite

American marines patrolled the streets of Hue during the Vietnam war. The city was occupied by the Viet Cong.

wall containing the names of more than fifty-eight thousand US citizens killed in the conflict. It was designed to bind the emotional wounds the country suffered, and it is sometimes called the "wall of healing." In his book *Marine Pride*, Marine Captain Scott Keller said,

> . . . there is a flag pole at [the wall's base containing] the seals of all the services: Army, Navy, Marines, Air Force, and Coast Guard. Every day throughout the year, a detachment from Marine Barracks Eighth & I marches to the flag and polishes the Marine Corps Emblem. The other services have never touched theirs. There is, perhaps, a lesson here.[7]

Attack on the Beirut Barracks

Marines are often deployed as "peacekeepers." In this capacity they attempt to stop civil wars and riots before they escalate and kill many innocent people. In September 1982, a Marine unit was sent to the Middle Eastern nation of Lebanon to help keep order in the face of civil strife. Marine units slept in a four-story concrete building near the Beirut, Lebanon, airport. Early on a Sunday morning, October 23, 1983, a truck crashed through the fence surrounding the building. The truck was driven by a suicide bomber. It rammed through the building's main door and into the lobby. In the bed of the truck were explosives equal to six tons of TNT. An incredible explosion tore apart the building, killing 241 Americans, 220 of them Marines.[8] It was a horrendous act of terrorism.

Operation Desert Storm

In July 1990, the Iraq leader Saddam Hussein invaded his neighbor, the oil-rich country of Kuwait. Iraqi troops occupied Kuwait despite the demands of the UN and other international authorities for them to withdraw. President George H. W. Bush sent American forces to other countries in the region. The forces of other nations joined them, and soon the Persian Gulf War began.

A full Marine expeditionary force, including infantry, tanks, helicopters, and fighter planes, participated in the Gulf War. Qualification requirements for joining the Corps had risen in recent years and the Persian Gulf War men and women reflected the new standards. These were the brightest, best-educated Marines ever sent to battle. Whereas only half the Vietnam-era Marines were high school graduates, almost 100 percent of the Gulf War Leathernecks had their diplomas. Intense training prepared the Marines for the desert warfare ahead.

The Iraqi air force was quickly neutralized, and the skies belonged to the American-led forces. Marine fighter planes worked closely with ground troops to eliminate Iraqi artillery. Marine General Mike Myatt said, "We convinced [the Iraqi artillery crews] it wasn't smart to man their artillery pieces because every time they did Marine air would come rolling in on them."[9]

On February 24, 1991, fast-moving columns of Marine tanks and armored troop carriers stormed into Iraqi positions. At the time, many Marine units were equipped with the aging M60 tank. This tank was considered inferior to the M1 Abrams tank used by the Army. No matter. Marine tankers performed brilliantly at the Burquan Oil Field during the largest tank battle of the Gulf War. In a heavy fog and amid smoke from dozens of oil fires, Marine tanks destroyed thirty-nine enemy vehicles.

US Marines arrive at Saudi Dhahran air base August 21, 1990, a few weeks after Iraq invaded Kuwait.

The ground operations of the Persian Gulf War lasted only two full days. American servicemen and women (all branches) suffered 370 killed. The Iraqi army may have lost up to one hundred thousand troops. Many thousands of Iraqi civilians—the true number will never be known—died under a rain of American bombs and missiles.

The Global War on Terrorism

September 11, 2001, is a day burned into the memory of all Americans. On that day, hijacked jetliners slammed into the World Trade Center twin towers and the Pentagon, and one crashed into a field in rural Pennsylvania. Almost three thousand people were killed that day.

Orchestrating this incredible act of terrorism was a shadowy group called Al-Qaeda. The group was led by a Saudi Arabian man named Osama bin Laden and his headquarters in the Asian country of Afghanistan.

Just days after the terrorist attacks, American special forces flew to Afghanistan and began the hunt for bin Laden. In late November, the first regular troops landed in this remote country. Those regulars were US Marines.

By December of that year, Marines from the 26th Marine Expeditionary Unit (MEU) captured the Kandahar Airport and established one of the first coalition command centers in the country. In 2010, the war in Afghanistan had become the longest war in US history. As of 2015, the United States still maintains a military presence in that country. Much progress has been made: the country held its first direct elections in 2004 and its first parliamentary elections in 2005, much of the territory has been reclaimed from the Taliban—including the stronghold of Marjah and bin Laden was killed in 2010.

Female US Marines patrol the streets in Musa Qala, Afghanistan, November 2010.

In March 2003, Marines and Army troops swept into Iraq for Operation Iraqi Freedom, and the ground war for that country began. The United States was supported by troops from Great Britain, Poland, and Australia. President George W. Bush ordered the war primarily because intelligence reports claimed the Iraqis owned weapons of mass destruction (WMDs). The president feared the Iraqi dictator, Saddam Hussein, would use those weapons on the United States and its allies. The WMDs included chemical and biological devices that could kill millions.

The ground war was violent but short. In just three weeks, American forces stormed into Baghdad, the capital of Iraq. It seemed the war in that country was over. However, the Americans never found any evidence that Iraqi forces had

The Lion of Fallujah: Major Douglas A. Zambiec

Awarded the Silver Star, the Bronze Star with Combat Distinguishing Device and two Purple Hearts for injuries sustained in combat during the Marines' ground assault into Fallujah as part of Operation Vigilant Resolve in 2004, Marine Major Douglas Zambiec's became a legend for his heroic actions during this bloody battle as the leader of Echo Company 2/1. He was tragically killed by small arms fire during a raid on his fourth combat tour in Iraq. General David Petraeus, who served as the Commanding General, Multi-National Force-Iraq, described Major Zambiec as "a true charter member of the brotherhood of the close fight."[10]

the dreaded WMDs. Later, the Bush administration admitted its prewar intelligence concerning the WMDs was flawed.

After the fall of Baghdad, a new war began. It was called an insurgency, or a war of occupation, depending on one's point of view. Die-hard supporters of Saddam Hussein and insurgents who had come from other Middle Eastern countries fought the Americans. Iraqi ethnic groups fought each other, and the Americans were often caught in the middle of their battles. Saddam Hussein himself was captured by soldiers on December 13, 2003, yet the war raged on. An insurgency quickly arose and a struggle for control of the country has ensued ever since. The First and Second Battles of Fallujah, both in 2004, were led by Marines and were intended to root out the insurgency stronghold in this city. The second battle proved to be the bloodiest involving American troops since the Vietnam War, but the American military was able to clear the city of most of the insurgents.

The war in Iraq officially ended in 2011 when the last US troops exited the country. However, part of the Al-Qaeda organization in Iraq split and began to re-invade Iraq's western provinces under the name of the Islamic State of Iraq and Syria (ISIS), taking over much of the country and combining the Iraq insurgency and the neighboring civil war in Syria into one conflict. President Obama authorized a series of air strikes against the rogue group of terrorists beginning in August 2014.

As of March 27, 2015, a total of 3,482 military personnel have been killed in action in Iraq and a total of 1,832 military personnel have been killed in action in Afghanistan.[11]

After the fighting ended, US Marines stayed on to ensure the safety of the Iraqi people.

Responding to Humanitarian Crises

Marines are not only first to fight, but they are also often the first Americans called upon to save lives on global missions. These missions are called MOOTWs, an acronym for Military Operations Other Than War. During the MOOTWs, men and women of the Corps are called upon to feed starving communities of civilians deprived of food due to civil strife. Marines also provide medical assistance when natural disasters such as earthquakes and tidal waves strike.

In December 1992, Marines landed on beaches in the African nation of Somalia. They were prepared to fight if necessary, but hoped to avoid gun battles. Somalia had been torn by civil war for years. Meanwhile, the people of the nation starved. The UN and other international agencies sent food, but it was looted by warring armies. The Marines were deployed as a police force. They protected food supplies and made sure food was properly distributed to hungry people. The Leathernecks accomplished their mission and hunger was eased in the troubled country. Fittingly, the Somalia MOOTW was called Operation Restore Hope.

Marines returned to Africa in June 1997, this time on a rescue mission to the country of Sierra Leone. A five-year-long civil war in Sierra Leone left thousands of people killed and wounded. A particularly brutal warring faction took over the country in 1997 and allowed its soldiers to loot stores and attack foreigners. The Marines took charge of this chaotic situation. Quickly, the Leathernecks evacuated foreigners, including a large group of Americans. Those rescued hailed the Marines as heroes.

In December 2004, a gigantic tidal wave, called a tsunami, washed over Pacific shores. The tsunami was one of the greatest disasters in human history. The great wall of water killed hundreds of thousands of people and left millions homeless. Marines joined other international forces to give medical assistance to the injured and to help restore order. On the island nation of Sri Lanka, Marine bulldozers rolled off naval ships. Immediately, the machines began to clear roads from debris and allow emergency supplies to reach cut-off villages. Said Gunnery Sergeant Juan Quijada of the 15th Marine Expeditionary Unit: "We'll be doing road-clearing projects and possibly airlift missions. We'll be here as long as we're needed. I hope it provides some relief to the people." Certainly the Sri Lankan people appreciated

After an 8.9-magnitude earthquake and tsunami devastated northern Japan in 2011, US Marines worked with the navy to conduct search-and-rescue operations and other relief missions.

the Marine efforts. Said one man: "The Americans are very helpful, not just to Sri Lanka but the world."[12]

The deadliest hurricane since 1928, Hurricane Katrina hit the Gulf Coast In 2005 with a vengeance and was the costliest natural disaster in this history of the United States. Once again, the Marines responded. They staged their operations at the Stennis International Airport in Bay St. Louis, Mississippi, and fanned out across the region in Amphibious Assault Vehicles (AAVs) through the flooded areas to rescue those stranded by the flooded areas. Once the water receded, the Marines also assisted in cleanup and rebuilding efforts in Mississippi and Louisiana.

In January 2010, a 7.0 earthquake hit Haiti, causing catastrophic damage to the population and the infrastructure of this island nation. Looting and violence ensued. In response, the Marines quickly deployed the 22nd and 24th Marine Expeditionary Units (MEUs) to provide security in a place that had become lawless. Amidst the disorder, the Marines also distributed 1.6 million rations of food, 560,000 liters of water and 15,000 pounds of medical supplies.

THE MARINE CORPS TODAY

There are only two kinds of people that understand Marines: Marines and the enemy. Everyone else has a second-hand opinion.

—Anonymous[1]

Their advertising campaign used to say: "The Few, The Proud, The Marines." With little more than 195,000 men and women serving on active duty, the United States Marine Corps is the smallest branch of the four major military services (Army, Navy and Air Force). Frequently called "America's 9-1-1 force," the Marines are our nation's amphibious, expeditionary, and air to ground logistics task force.

Members of the Corps can be stationed anywhere in the world. Marines stand guard at all US embassies. Hawaii and Japan have large Marine contingents. A majority of all Marines are assigned to the Corps' three infantry divisions. These infantry divisions make up the Fleet Marine Force (FMF). The divisions are strategically stationed around the world. The 1st Marine Division is headquartered at Camp Pendleton near Oceanside, California. The 2nd Division is at Camp Lejeune near Jacksonville, North Carolina. The 3rd Division is on Okinawa, Japan.

Marines remain soldiers of the sea. Leathernecks still specialize in amphibious, ship-to-shore warfare. In this capacity, the Corps works closely with the Navy. Experts agree that waging amphibious war is the most difficult and dangerous of all large-scale military missions.

Marine training includes intense conditioning such as this long hike at Camp Pendleton, California.

The Corps has its own aviation contingent. Marine air units are divided into three air wings. Each air wing is attached to an infantry division. Marine pilots fly fighter planes similar to those used in the Navy. In combat, the fighter planes provide close support to ground troops. The Corps also maintains a large fleet of helicopters.

Marine Corps Reserves

Almost 40,000 men and women serve in the Marine Reserves. They are divided into three groups: the Ready Reserve, the Standby Reserve, and the Retired Reserve. Members of the Ready Reserve train one weekend a month and serve two weeks of full-time duty each year. Ready Reservists are the first to be called into active duty if the need arises. The Standby Reserve is made up of those who have already served on active duty. The Standby men and women do not have weekend training obligations, but they may also be ordered into duty in times of emergencies. Retired Reserves are those who have served twenty years or more in the Corps and are

"Semper Fi": The Marine Motto

The Marine motto is almost sacred to members of the Corps: *Semper Fidelis*, Latin words for "Always Faithful." A shortened version of the motto is "Semper Fi." This is a common greeting or a way of saying farewell among Marines. Letters and e-mail sent by Marines often end with "Semper Fi."

now collecting pensions. Even the Retired Reserve can be pressed into emergency duty.

Newspaper writers sometimes call the Ready Reservists "part-time Marines" or "weekend warriors." These names fail to do them justice. All members of the Ready Reserve know they can be called up with a few days' notice and find themselves on active duty overseas shortly after the call-up.

A typical reserve unit is the helicopter squadron HMLA 773, nicknamed Task Force Red Dog. The Red Dogs, as they call themselves, are from Georgia and Louisiana. All are established in their civilian careers. One is a pilot for Federal Express and another is an FBI agent. The squadron, which consists of three hundred men and nine helicopters, was activated in 2004 and sent to Afghanistan. Certainly these servicemembers missed their families. But they were Marines and they joined in the hunt for the master terrorist Osama bin Laden.

For six months the Red Dogs served in Afghanistan. While supporting ground troops, they flew helicopters through snowstorms and through thick fog. Several times, helicopters from the Red Dog Squadron engaged in firefights with Afghan rebels on the ground. Finally, the squadron was allowed to go home. But there the Reservists received depressing news. The squadron's active duty assignment was extended twelve months, and they were due to return to Afghanistan.

The Marine Corps Commandant

The Marines' highest-ranking officer is a four-star general called the Commandant of the Marine Corps. In 2015, the commandant was General Joseph F. Dunford, Jr., a

Members of the US Marine Red Dog Task Force conduct Marine Corps martial arts training. The Red Dogs are a helicopter squadron unit in the Marines.

native of Boston, Massachusetts, and a graduate from St. Michael's College. General Dunford previously served as the Commander, International Security Assistance Force and United States Forces-Afghanistan. General Dunford has served as an infantry officer at all levels. He commanded 2nd Battalion, 6th Marines, and during Operation Iraqi Freedom, he commanded the 5th Marine Regiment.

The commandant is appointed by the president of the United States. He holds the office for four years. Dunford is the thirty-sixth Commandant of the Marine Corps. The first commandant was Samuel Nicholas who served from 1775 to 1781.

Several famous commandants have risen to almost legendary status in Marine lore. Archibald Henderson, the fifth commandant, served from 1820 to 1859. No other commandant had a longer tenure than Henderson. For that reason, Henderson is called "the old man of the Marine Corps." John Archer Lejeune, the thirteenth commandant, led the Corps from 1920 to 1929. Lejeune saw combat in World War I and later developed amphibious warfare doctrine that was used by the Corps in World War II. The huge base in North Carolina, Camp Lejeune, is named for this memorable commandant. Alexander Archer "Archie" Vandergrift, the eighteenth commandant, was the top Marine from 1944 to 1947. Early in World War II, Vandergrift commanded the 1st Marine Division on the assault of Guadalcanal. For his

Marine Corps Reserves' "Toys for Tots" Campaign

A well-known charity run by the Marine Corps Reserves is the holiday Toys for Tots program. Beginning in 1947, reservists started collecting used toys and distributing them to needy children. Today, reserve units all over the country gather new toys in unopened boxes for distribution. Every holiday season, some 7 million children benefit from the Marine Reserves' Toys for Tots drive.

staunch defense of that island in the face of repeated enemy attacks, Vandergrift won the Medal of Honor.

The Marine Corps Band

Stationed permanently in Washington is the Marine Band. Consisting of roughly 160 members, it is the most famous military band in the United States. It is called "The President's Own" because it performs at all ceremonies concerning the nation's chief executive. The band traces its history back to the administration of Thomas Jefferson.

Band members are technically enlisted Marines. However, band personnel receive no rifle training nor are they sent to Marine boot camp. Those chosen for the Marine Band are music majors selected from the nation's best colleges. Many

Archibald Henderson

hold doctorates and master's degrees in their specialties. They play with spirit and technical precision. Experts regard the President's Own Band as one of the greatest military bands in the world.

Easily the most famous Marine Band leader was John Philip Sousa, who presided over the group from 1880 to 1892. Sousa grew up in Washington and loved band music. As a young boy, he was tempted

The United States Marine Band marches in during the National Cherry Blossom Festival and Parade in Washington, D.C.

to run away and join a circus band. Instead, he took over the Marine Band and led it to world fame. Called the "March King," Sousa composed some of the most stirring marches ever written: "Semper Fidelis," "The Washington Post," "El Capitan," and "The Stars and Stripes Forever." Sousa's music is still performed and loved all over the world. He always strove to perfect his organization. Sousa once wrote, "the Marine Band is the national band . . . as great among bands as America is among nations."[2]

The official home of the Marine Band is the historic Marine Barracks on the corner of 8th and I Streets in Washington. Built in 1806, it is known as the "oldest post in the Corps." The barracks building also houses the Commandant's Own Drum and Bugle Corps. A popular show for tourists and Washingtonians alike is the Evening Parade. This parade is a seventy-five-minute performance played out on Friday evenings at 8:45 during the summer months. The parade features the Marine Band, the Marine Drum and Bugle Corps, and the Marine Corps Silent Drill Platoon. It is free and open to the public, but reservations are suggested.

The US Marine Corps Silent Drill Platoon performs as the Blue Angels soar above them at the Marine Corps Air Station in Yuma, Arizona.

CHAPTER 6

SO YOU WANT TO BE A MARINE?

This is my rifle. There are many like it, but this one is mine.
My rifle is my best friend. It is my life. I must master it as I master my life.

—The opening lines of "This Is My Rifle," which is recited by all Marine trainees. "This Is My Rifle" was written in 1942 by General William H. Rupertus.[1]

The Marine Corps is an exclusive club. They set high standards for new club members to join. Some are turned away because they scored low on standardized tests. Others fail to qualify for physical reasons. So, it is important to know that any high school graduate who wants to join the Marine Corps has to reach a high bar.

So You Want to Be a Marine?

In order to apply for enlistment, a person must be between eighteen and twenty-eight years of age. The Corps will reject anyone who has been convicted of a major crime. However, candidates who have had a minor brush with the law can be accepted. A high school diploma is not a requirement, but far more than 90 percent of Marine enlistees have completed high school. One must be in excellent physical condition to gain admission. Candidates cannot use drugs.

Enlisting

Think of the Corps as an exclusive club. The Marines set high standards for new club members to join. Many young applicants are rejected for various reasons. Some are turned down because they scored low on intelligence tests. Others fail to qualify for physical reasons. Some are tuned down because of their tattoos. Despite the lofty qualification standards, the Marines usually fill their ranks with ample recruits. Many young people interested in the military want to join what they consider to be the best branch.

For many years the United States relied on the draft to fill its military ranks. In theory, the draft required all young men to serve at least some time in one of the military branches. The country has never drafted women. There were many exceptions made in the actual practice of the draft. College students could delay their service duties and even avoid them altogether by simply staying in school. These exceptions led to the bitter charge that the draft system was unfair. Rich young men who could afford to remain in college escaped going to war while poor young men were routinely sent to the fighting fronts. The United States ended the draft in 1973. The country now has an all-volunteer military. However, the

Recruits can enlist in the Marines at a Marine Corps recruiting office like this one in Belle Vernon, Pennsylvania.

Selective Service still exists. All men must register with the Selective Service upon reaching the age of eighteen.

Reporting for Duty

All right. You have been accepted into the Marine Corps. Congratulations! Now comes the hard part: a three-month training program called boot camp.

"Sir, yessir! Sir, the recruit's name is . . ."

"I can't HEAR you."

"Sir, yessir! Sir the recruit's name . . ."

You better get used to this sort of talk—shouted at the top of your lungs—if you want to survive Marine Corps boot camp. The aim of boot camp is to diminish your individuality and make you part of a unit. You do not even use the simple pronouns "I" or "me" because those words reflect individuality. Instead, you stand at stiff attention and yell, "Sir, the recruit does not know how to disassemble the M16A2 rifle, sir!" or, "Sir, the recruit will obey all orders, sir!" To further repress individual expressions and pleasures, male recruits are given a "buzz cut," a haircut down to the scalp. The buzz cut makes the young men look at least somewhat alike. Females are allowed to keep their hair, but it must be cut close and kept neat.

Learning to Talk Like a Marine

After a few weeks of boot camp, the recruit begins to speak a new language: Marine Talk. Many Marine terms come from the Navy—a floor is a "deck," a wall is a "bulkhead," and the bathroom is a "head." However, some expressions are purely Marine. Here are some widely used Marine expressions and terms:

field day—A day when everyone pitches in to give the barracks a vigorous scrubbing.

gung ho—Words used to describe Marine enthusiasm; the term comes from a 1943 movie.

scuttlebutt—Rumors; a scuttlebutt is also a drinking fountain, a place where rumors are discussed.

squared away—A particularly neat and tidy Marine is said to be "squared away."

ooooo-rah—This is a battle cry that Marines began using shortly after the Vietnam War. No one knows its origin, but it is similar to the Russian army's World War II battle cry: uuuuu-rah.

The Marine Corps maintains two boot camps, also called Marine Corps Recruit Depots (MCRDs). One MCRD is at San Diego, California, and it trains male recruits who enlist from homes west of the Mississippi River. The other MCRD is at Parris Island, South Carolina, and it receives male recruits from states east of the Mississippi. All female recruits are sent to Parris Island regardless of where they live. Men and women recruits get almost the same training. During basic training, men and women are housed in separate barracks and work in separate units. In boot camp, there is little mixing of the sexes.

Training routine at the two camps is identical. Yet the Parris Island graduates claim their experience is more intense because they cope with the heat and the biting sand fleas in South Carolina. PI Marines call their San Diego counterparts "Hollywood Marines" for the base's California location. It is impossible to determine, really, which is the toughest boot camp. Still, the arguments between PI and San Diego have raged in Marine barracks for well more than fifty years.

Why these training bases are called boot camps is another legend of the Corps. One story says that in the old days, the first item issued to a recruit was a pair of boots. Therefore, MCRDs were always called boot camps. Whatever the origin of the name, boot camp is a basic training facility. All branches of the service require basic training for new enlistees. But no other basic training program is tougher than Marine boot camp.

Life for a recruit centers around his or her platoon. The platoon has eighty members. Each platoon is run by four sergeants who are called drill instructors (DIs). The DI is a demanding boss, a parent figure, and a teacher all forged into

Female Marine recruits go through pugil stick training at boot camp at the Marine Corps Recruit Depot at Parris Island, South Carolina.

one rock-hard Marine. Under the eyes of the DI, recruits learn to march with the M16 rifle. Recruits also disassemble their rifles, meticulously clean them, and memorize the proper names of each tiny part. In a few weeks, a recruit can take the rifle apart and put it back together again blindfolded.

The DI is also a physical education instructor and leads the platoon in vigorous exercise sessions. All recruits must pass a basic test that includes three pull-ups, forty sit-ups performed in two minutes, and a three-mile run completed in twenty-eight minutes. Not everyone can keep up with the rigorous program. A small number of men and women recruits are dismissed from the Corps for various reasons during the three months of boot camp. Perhaps the recruits cannot meet the physical demands of marching and vigorous exercise. Some recruits break down psychologically and are released from boot camp.

Food in boot camp is good and plentiful because it is important to eat properly in order to endure the physical demands of training. However, if a recruit is overweight, he or she is given a "diet tray" with low-fat and low-calorie foods. Those who are underweight are fed extra rations. Building strength and toughness is a boot camp goal.

Week six is devoted to weapons training. Recruits "snap in," meaning they practice various firing positions without actually discharging their rifles. Target shooting is next. Young Marines are given points and grades for the accuracy they achieve: 190 points earns a Marksman's badge, 210 a Sharpshooter, and 220 an Expert. Recruits are also taught to shoot either right-handed or left-handed and to fire their rifle while wearing a gas mask.

The ultimate physical challenge facing recruits comes in the final week with an ordeal called the Crucible. For fifty-four hours recruits endure live firing and close combat exercises. All these training duties require close cooperation between platoon members. In one cooperation drill, recruits deliberately fall backward into the waiting arms of their fellow platoon members. The men get only four hours of sleep and are fed limited rations. The Crucible is capped off with a brisk nine-mile hike with rifles and full packs. In San Diego, the hiking trail leads up a killer hill called, appropriately, the Grim Reaper.

So You Want to Be a Marine?

Recruits handle weapons on an obstacle course during the Crucible at the combat training area on Parris Island. The Crucible is a grueling training challenge that recruits must pass before boot camp graduation.

Two rewards await the recruit finishing the Crucible: First, the recruit is served a "warrior's breakfast" consisting of steak, eggs, and pancakes. Second, the recruit receives the official Marine Corps Emblem—the globe and anchor—to wear on his or her collar. The emblem is a badge of honor.

Graduation from boot camp is marked with a full dress parade. Men and women graduates have paid in sweat, pain, and perhaps a few tears to take their place on this parade ground. As the band plays "The Marine Corps Hymn," the

US Marine recruits learn basic swimming techniques at boot camp.

A platoon marches in advance of graduation ceremonies at Parris Island. Once recruits make it through the Crucible they are rewarded with graduation and a full dress parade.

boot camp survivors know they are Marines now—and they will be for the rest of their lives.

The Officers Corps

Young officers signing up with the Corps come from the nation's colleges and universities. Some future lieutenants are graduates of the US Naval Academy at Annapolis, Maryland. Still other officers-to-be are recruited from the Corps' enlisted ranks.

Officers comprise less than 10 percent of all Marine personnel.[2] For every eight enlisted men and women there is one officer. The other four military branches have a far greater percentage of officers in their ranks.[3] In the Marines, senior enlisted men (noncommissioned officers, called NCOs) assume a greater leadership role.

Officers do not go to boot camp. Instead, they attend Officer Candidate School (OCS) in Quantico, Virginia. In many respects, OCS is as physically demanding as boot camp. The future second lieutenants learn to march and fire weapons. The motto of OCS is *Ductus Exemplo* (Leadership by Example). This means the junior officers must be willing to do all the tasks and take all the risks expected of the enlisted men and women. Soon, graduates of OCS will lead a platoon in the field. Perhaps they will be in a combat situation shortly after their OCS experience. They are expected to set sound examples to command the respect of the enlisted ranks.

OCS is a ten-week course. As is true with boot camp, the officer candidates march, study Marine Corps history and traditions, and fire weapons. At the end, the officers endure their own version of the Crucible. In a five-day program called "War Week," they work under simulated combat conditions while learning to lead men into battle. After OCS, officers attend the Basic School, six more months of intense physical training. All young lieutenants come to understand that a Marine officer is a leader who is entrusted with the lives of fellow Marines.

MARINE TRAINING

We have answered the call and we have delivered! Throughout the last decade, Marines have enhanced their reputation as the Nation's premier force in readiness. Today's Marines, like their predecessors, can be very proud to claim the title United States Marine.

—General Joseph F. Dunford Jr., Commandant of the Marine Corps, writing in 2013[1]

The Marine Corps has been serving on the frontlines in the fight against terrorism around the world. Any man or woman who wants to volunteer to join this team of elite warriors will start their service with boot camp. Boot camp takes place at one of two places, Marine Corps Recruit Depot (MCRD) Parris Island, South Carolina or MCRD San Diego. Every recruit begins their transformation into a Marine by standing on two legendary yellow footprints, as they are given their first directions from a drill instructor (DI). The DI explains the Uniform Code of Military Justice, the recruits are issued gear and given a medical evaluation, and then start the challenging twelve-week journey to earn the title "Marine."

Upon graduation from boot camp, a Marine is sent to the School of Infantry. This is a fifty-two-day course of intense combat training. The first fourteen days at the special school are devoted to what is called a Common Skills Package. Here a Marine learns how to detect and fire at targets in the field. Such field firing is a new concept as opposed to target shooting on the rifle range in boot camp. Also in the School of Infantry, Marines learn deadly tasks such as hand grenade throwing and disarming land mines.

After completing the Combat Skills course, male Marines branch off to become specialists in infantry weapons. The men learn how to fire and maintain machine guns, mortars, and antitank guided missiles. Female Marines take the Combat Skills Package, but they do not train in special infantry weapons. By law, women are forbidden on fighting fronts during combat. Therefore, it is deemed unnecessary to teach female Marines special weapons skills.

Once they have completed the School of Infantry, most Marines will be assigned to one of the three infantry divisions. There they will need no reminder that the Marine's primary job is to carry a rifle into battle. The infantry divisions constantly train so they will be ready for combat assignments.

New boot camp graduates head to the School of Infantry. These Marines are ready to go on a night march during Marine Combat Training.

The Marine's Rifle

Marines enter combat with the M16 rifle. Versions of the M16 have been employed by the Marine Corps for more than thirty years. At first the rifle was cursed because it frequently jammed up in the field and failed to fire. Through the years, the rifle has been refined and improved. It now functions very well under all conditions—from tropical jungles to the snows of northern lands. The rifle can be fired semiautomatically (each trigger pull discharges one bullet) or it can be fired in bursts of three rounds. The M16A2 is 39.63 inches long and weights 8.79 pounds with a 30-round magazine.

Marine sniper teams are the specialists responsible for covering long-range targets during ground combat missions. In 2002, the Marines added a Designated Marksman to its sniper teams to increase the effectiveness of the teams in covering mid- to short-range targets. These Marksmen use an M14 automatic rifle or an M16 assault rifle with a telescopic sight to reach targets at two to five hundred yards.

The Infantry's Weapons

The infantry would be at a serious disadvantage without supporting weapons such as artillery, tanks, and armored personnel carriers. The Fleet Marine Force relies on amphibious craft to get the infantry from ships to shores. Such highly technical vehicles and weapons require their own specialists to keep them in operation.

Artillery pieces propel high explosive shells long distances into enemy-held positions. The mainstay of Marine artillery is the 155 mm Howitzer. Most are towed weapons, meaning they are pulled by a truck. The latest version of the 155 is called the M777E1. This new edition of the 155 fires

Rifle Training

All Marines must become familiar with the Squad Automatic Weapon (SAW). The SAW fires automatically like a machine gun. At 15 pounds the SAW is easily carried by one Marine. It uses either a 30-round magazine or a 200-round plastic package. Marines have employed such weapons since the days of the Browning Automatic Rifle (BAR), which was developed before World War II.

Marine Reconnaissance

If Marines are the best infantry troops in the world (and they believe they are), a small group called Force Recon can be hailed as the best of the best. Force Recon is an outgrowth of the Marine reconnaissance companies that once scouted the terrain far ahead of advancing infantry units. Today, members of the Force Recon endure the most physically demanding training in the Marine Corps. Recon men practice parachute jumping as well as underwater diving. They are sent on grueling hikes. They learn to find their way over difficult terrain in day or night. All are volunteers.

the same high explosive shell, but is six thousand pounds lighter than the old model. Loading and firing artillery pieces requires intense teamwork. A well-drilled squad moves with the precision of ballet dancers as they pass the rounds forward, make gun correction, and fire. Experienced crews on a 155 can shoot four shells a minute.

Today, Marines still specialize in ship-to-shore assaults. During World War II and Korea, that meant taking the slow-moving, lightly armored amtracs into battle. World War II men are shocked when they look at today's seagoing assault vehicles. Long ago, the Amphibious Assault Vehicle (AAV) replaced the World War II-era amtrac. Modern AAVs have armor plating, and they carry up to twenty-one combat-loaded Marines. On land the AAVs travel at twenty to thirty miles an hour. But the AAV moves only about six miles an hour in the water. The latest assault vehicle is the Landing Craft Air Cushion (LCAC). Riding on a cushion of air, the LCAC can carry a six-hundred-ton payload over the waves at the astonishing speed of almost fifty miles per hour. Air cushions, formed by huge propellers, allow the LCAC to skirt up a beach and give the Marines aboard a dry foot landing.

It is the Marines' job to land on hostile shores. It is the Navy's job to get them there. The Navy uses special amphibious assault ships to take Marines to their assigned beaches. The USS *Tarawa* and the USS *Wasp* are examples of assault ships used to transport Marines. The vessels resemble aircraft carriers. They are almost three football fields in length. Helicopters and light fighter planes take off from their flat decks. The Marines live below decks until they are called upon to board helicopters and landing craft for the assault. The landing craft are housed in the "well decks" of the amphibious ships, which are then flooded to allow the landing craft to exit the ship and travel across the ocean. Thus, the ships allow Marines to approach enemy shores through the air or over the waves. Sometimes the ships that make up the amphibious assault fleet are called "Gator Freighters" and the fleet is known as the "Gator Navy."

Though Marines are a light infantry force, they use the nation's heaviest tank. Fully loaded, the M1A1 Main Battle Tank (used by the Army as well as the Marine Corps) weighs 67.7 tons. It is armed with a powerful 120 mm gun that is aimed with the aid of electronic devices. The accuracy of this gun is amazing. It can hit a target more than 2.5 miles away. The M1A1 has a crew of four: a driver, a gunner, a loader, and the commander. It is hailed as the best tank in the world.

The primary light armored vehicle for the Marines is Light Armored Vehicle-25 (LAV-25). This is an armored personnel carrier propelled by eight wheels. The vehicle is sometimes called a "battle taxi" because it drives men to the fighting fronts. It has a crew of three and is capable of carrying six troops. Weighing twenty-four thousand pounds, the LAV-25 can reach sixty miles per hour on the ground. As an amphibious vehicle, it runs at about six miles per hour on the water. The LAV-25 is armed with a 25 mm chain gun and a 7.62 mm machine gun.

To defeat enemy tanks and armored personnel carriers, the Marines employ a lethal device called the Dragon. A shoulder-held weapon, the Dragon can be the Marine's best friend in combat. The tube-shaped device weighs forty-eight pounds. Ground troops simply aim the Dragon at enemy vehicles and fire. Its round has a special charge that enables it to penetrate thick armor. The Dragon can destroy a thirty-five-ton tank. An older antitank weapon called the TOW is also used by the Corps.

Marine Aviation

Marine aircraft may be divided into three categories: fixed-wing, rotary wing, and—the newest model—tilt rotor. All three types operate from ships or from land.

Fixed-wing planes include swift fighters and dive bombers. The primary Marine fighter plane is the F/A-18D Hornet. This twin-jet aircraft clears enemy planes from the skies and provides ground support for Marine infantry. The Hornet is capable of reaching speeds up to 1,100 miles per hour. The plane has a 20 mm cannon mounted in its nose and it can carry thirteen thousand pounds of bombs or

These US Marines are on a mission to intercept Taliban forces in the Helmand province in Afghanistan.

Fred Smith: Marine and Founder of FedEx

As the founder, chairman, president, and chief executive officer of FedEx (formerly Federal Express), Fred Smith conceived the idea for the overnight delivery company while writing a paper for his college economics class in the 1960s. But many people do not know that his first job was as a Marine. He was commissioned an officer in 1966, serving for three years as a platoon leader and as a forward air controller (FAC). He served two tours in Vietnam, flying with pilots on over 200 combat missions. It was during his time in the Marines that he was able to observe the military's logistics and delivery procedures and where he fine-tuned his dream to create what has become the first and largest overnight express delivery company in the world.

missiles. Hornets can operate either from aircraft carriers or from advanced land bases.

Another fixed-wing aircraft used by the Corps is the AV-8B Harrier II. The Harrier is slow by jet standards (its maximum speed is about 660 miles per hour). However, the Harrier has a unique way of directing its jet exhaust downward. This downward thrust enables the plane to take off vertically like a helicopter. Short take-off and landing requirements make the Harrier particularly useful in Marine ship-to-shore operations. The Harrier can also hover in the air, fly backwards, or fly in a tight circle.

Marines use two primary types of helicopters: those designed to attack ground targets and those made to transport troops or cargo. Helicopters are called rotary wing aircraft because their propellers are in fact wings that rotate.

The attack helicopter is basically a gunship. Attack helicopters fire on enemy ground troops with machine guns or with rockets. The latest Marine attack helicopter is the AH-1W Super Cobra. This helicopter carries a 20mm cannon with 750 rounds of ammunition. Manned by a crew of two officers, it is also armed with rockets and a wide variety of precision-guided missiles. Some missiles mounted on Cobras are designed to shoot down enemy helicopters. The Cobra is capable of reaching speeds of 160 miles per hour. In the 1991 Iraq War, Cobras destroyed almost one hundred Iraqi tanks.

Transport helicopters speed troops on various missions. In combat conditions, most transport helicopters will be armed with an auxiliary machine gun. An important Marine transport helicopter is the CH-46E Sea Knight. The Sea Knight has a crew of four and can carry fourteen combat-loaded marines. Its maximum speed is 160 miles per hour. The Sea Knight can be used to evacuate wounded Marines. In such cases, it becomes a first aid station in the sky. When doing medical evacuation work, the Sea Knight can carry up to fifteen stretcher cases and two attendants.

A true workhorse as a cargo-carrying helicopter is the CH-53E Super Stallion. This mighty rotary winged aircraft has a crew of four. Almost seventy thousand pounds of equipment or cargo can be stuffed into the Super Stallion's huge interior.

An old favorite among Marine pilots is the UH-1N Huey Helicopter. A versatile craft, the Huey can be fitted for various missions. Versions of the Huey have served the Marines since the 1960s.

The Marines' latest troop-carrying aircraft is the MV-22 Osprey. It is a tilt rotor plane, combining the qualities of rotary wing and fixed-wing designs. The Osprey has two rotors mounted on a wing. For takeoffs, the rotors and wing are pointed upward. This allows the craft to rise like a helicopter. In the air, the wings and the rotors are shifted to the level position so the Osprey can fly like a fixed-wing airplane. The rotor and wing shift takes just twelve seconds to complete.

The advantages to the Osprey design are obvious. Carrying twenty-four infantrymen, the Osprey takes off

A Marine practices how to land in a virtual parachute simulator as part of safety and survival training for fixed wing aircraft.

straight up like a helicopter. In level flight, it flies like an airplane. It is twice as fast and has twice the range of the average helicopter. The Osprey, however, is a new concept in aviation. It became operational in 2007 and has become a favorite for all kind of missions, including carrying freight, medical transport, and enemy assaults where it carries loads of Marines into and out of combat landing zones. Twice as fast as its predecessor, the CH-46 Sea Knight, the V-22 Osprey has a longer range, and can carry more cargo and more than twice as many troops.

Drones

The official Marine digest, *Concepts and Programs*, reads, "In Iraq, battles are won on intelligence first, bullets second."[2] Bearing that concept in mind, the Corps has developed several unmanned aerial vehicles (UAVs) more commonly called "drones." These robotic aircraft serve as eyes in the air. Flying without a pilot, they relay television pictures of enemy movements back to ground commanders. Some UAVs are small and look much like model aircraft. The most up-to-date spy aircraft is called Eagle Eye. A tilt-wing UAV, the Eagle Eye penetrates far and high to spy on the enemy. Many UAVs are so small they do not appear on enemy radar. They can readily be sent into "hot spots" without risking the life of a pilot.

Support and Supply Vehicles

Not all Marine vehicles are designed to operate directly on battlefronts. The Corps uses trucks and cars for the everyday tasks of hauling food to camps or carting garbage out of camps. These ordinary vehicles are not as exciting as front-line transports, but they play a vital role.

The Dragon Eye, a drone, can fly into enemy territory for one hour to take infrared real time images. This saves Marines from entering potentially dangerous situations.

A vehicle seen in all units is the High Mobility Multipurpose Wheeled Vehicle (HMMWV), popularly called the Humvee. A rugged small truck, the Humvee can traverse over rough country where there are no roads. It can be fitted to play a variety of roles. Humvees act as ambulances, antitank missile launchers, and troop carriers.

The Iraq War brought out a weakness in the Humvee. The light truck has no armor protection. Marines often patrol in hostile territory aboard Humvees. Patrols took terrible casualties when the vehicle struck a land mine, an Improvised Explosive Device (IED), or was hit by rocket-propelled grenades. Clever Marine engineers welded scrap metal to the Humvee's sides to protect against grenade attacks. Later Humvees arriving in Iraq were equipped with armor protection.

The most common truck seen in the Corps is the seven-ton truck. These trucks transport troops, ammunition, and supplies. They also pull trailers and light artillery guns. Maximum payload for this vehicle is 30,000 pounds when traveling over roads and 15,000 pounds when driving cross-country. They are not amphibious, meaning they cannot "swim" across water. But a special folding kit that extends the exhaust pipe and the air intake allows the truck to cross a river up to seven feet deep.

Marines employ a wide variety of specialized trucks and other vehicles. A huge truck called Container Transport Rear Body Unit can carry a payload of about 22.5 tons. Another heavy truck is the Recovery/Wrecker Body Unit. It is designed to tow damaged vehicles to repair shops. The wrecker is equipped with a derrick and can pull vehicles off the road in minutes. Smallest of the service vehicles is the KLR 250-D8 Marine Corps Motorcycle. Weighing 258 pounds, the motorcycle is used to speed maps and other documents from unit to unit.

The Commandant's Car

When he is in Washington, the Commandant of the Marine Corps rides in a civilian limousine painted in Marine green. Unique to the commandant's car is the license plate number—1775, the year the Marine Corps was born.

THE MARINE CORPS FAMILY

The personal ties between a Marine and his Corps are strong. Marines believe in their Corps. They also believe that they are the best. They insist the "M" in "Marine" be capitalized. The highest accolade they can bestow on a member of another service is "He would make a good Marine."

—Edward M. Simmons, Marine Brigadier General (retired) and historian, writing in 1997[1]

Since the Marine Corps is so small, it likes to think of itself as a family—working together to get a job done, but taking care of each other.

As is true in the rest of the nation, the Marines thrive in their diversity. America's strength comes from different racial and ethnic groups working together. Marines derive their strength from the same source. But this was not always the case. In the distant past, the Marine Corps was made up entirely of white males. Now the Marine family embraces all races and genders.

Women in the Marine Corps

For years the Marines were reluctant to take women into their ranks. The first small unit of women Marines served in World War I and were used as clerks. After the First World War, women were banned from the Corps. During World War II, women reentered the Marines. The women joined the ranks despite the misgivings of older officers and enlisted men. A story was told that when the wartime Marine Corps announced it would take women recruits, a strange event took place. Immediately after the announcement, a portrait of the legendary Commandant Archibald Henderson fell off the wall at Marine headquarters in Washington. Of course, this portrait calamity is only a story.

Some nineteen thousand women Marines served in World War II.[2] They did not see action on combat fronts during the war. But those who thought the Corps was no place for females were proven wrong. Women Marines became cryptologists, puzzling out the enemy's decoded messages. Some were typists and stenographers. Still other World War II women Marines worked as truck mechanics.

Today, women make up about 6 percent of the total Marine force. This 6 percent figure is far lower than the number of women in the other major services. (The Air

Force is comprised of 19.1percent women, the Army 13.6 percent, and the Navy 16.4 percent.[3]) That may change, however. In 2013, then-Secretary of Defense Leon Panetta announced a groundbreaking decision to overturn a 1994 rule that restricted women from artillery, armor, infantry and other such combat roles, opening up thousands of front-line positions that women had previously been barred from performing. The first three women graduated from the Marine Corps infantry training in November 2013.

In many modern conflicts, the policy of keeping women away from combat zones is difficult to enforce. The war in Iraq is a guerrilla war. It has no clearly defined battle lines. Everyone stationed anywhere in Iraq can be killed or wounded by a car bomb or by an enemy rocket or grenade. Women Marines in Iraq do not serve side by side with men

Brigadier General Loretta Reynolds

When she took command of Marine Corps Recruit Depot (MCRD) Parris Island in 2011, Brigadier General Loretta Reynolds was one of only two active duty female generals in the Marine Corps and the first female base commander of Parris Island. She is a 1986 graduate of the US Naval Academy and has commanded Marines in numerous locations, including Okinawa, Japan; Quantico, Virginia; Iraq; and Afghanistan. She is the first female Marine to hold a command position in a battle zone.

Women Marines on the Lioness Team are briefed at the start of training in Iraq. The Lioness program is an all-female search program that has been trained to be culturally sensitive when searching Iraqi and Muslim women.

on combat patrols. However, the women still face grave dangers even if they work at a field hospital or direct civilian traffic.

Minorities in the Marines

A regulation written in 1798 said, "No Negro, mulatto, or Indian" may join the Marine Corps.[4] Throughout its early history, membership in the Marines was restricted to whites only. Latinos and American Indians were allowed to join before World War II. African Americans were admitted into the Corps in 1942, but they were put in segregated units. In 1947, President Harry Truman signed an order forbidding segregation in all branches of the armed forces. The Marines were slow to integrate their ranks. However, by the early 1950s, blacks, whites, Hispanics, and other ethnic groups served together as equals in all units.

In the segregated Marine Corps of World War II, a legendary Marine named Gilbert H. Johnson rose to prominence. Johnson had served in the Army. When he came to the Marine Corps in 1942, he was promoted to field sergeant major and was put in charge of all African-American drill instructors. Johnson made certain that African-American members of the Corps had the best basic training the services could provide.

Frank E. Petersen entered the Corps in October 1952 and became one of a handful of African-American Marine pilots. Petersen flew combat missions in the Korean War and in Vietnam. In 1979, Frank Petersen was the first African-American Marine to be promoted to general.

While the commandant is the top Marine officer, the Corps also reveres its senior-enlisted man. In 2015, that

Diversity in the Marine Corps

According to the official *Marine Corps Almanac*, the racial figures of the active duty 2015 Marine Corps stood as follows:

Officers	Approximate Salary*
White	16,529
Black	1,159
Hispanic	1,340
Other	1,536
Total	20,564
Enlisted	
White	125,161
Hispanic	30,822
Black	19,848
Other	9,872
Total	185,703[5]

honor went to Sergeant Major Ronald L. Green. As the highest-ranking enlisted man, Green has the title sergeant major of the Marine Corps. A native of Jackson, Mississippi, Sergeant Green enlisted in 1983 and served in many capacities including as a drill instructor in Marine Boot Camp. On February 20, 2015, he was the eighteenth person granted the title sergeant major of the Marine Corps.

Marine Lieutenant Billy Mills is a Sioux Indian who was born on the Pine Ridge Reservation in 1938. Lieutenant Mills was an outstanding Marine officer. He was also an outstanding long-distance runner. In 1964, he went to the

The Marine Corps Family

Seargent Major Ronald L. Green is the Marine Corps' highest ranking noncomissioned officer. Green began his Marine life at Parris Island in 1983.

Olympic Games in Tokyo, Japan, to compete in the 10,000-meter run (a little over eight miles). No one gave the Marine lieutenant a chance to win. Americans at the time simply were not distance runners. The 10,000-meter race had never been won by an American athlete. Sioux pride and Marine pride motivated Lieutenant Billy Mills. He shocked the experts by winning the race and bringing home the Olympic gold medal. In 1983, a movie called *Running Brave* was made to celebrate his achievement.

Gays in the Marine Corps

The Marine Corps (and the entire Department of Defense) acknowledges that many homosexuals have served honorably and with distinction over the course of the nation's history, but gay men and women were prohibited from openly serving until 2010, when the ban on gays serving in the military was removed. All gay and bisexual men and women can now serve openly in all branches of the military.

The Life of a Marine: Study and Change

A Marine is never finished with school. Boot camp can be thought of as grade school. The fifty-two-day School of Infantry is the Marine equivalent of high school. Beyond that, Marines are likely to be assigned to one of dozens of schools to learn specialized skills. Even men and women who have been in the Corps for more than fifteen years can look forward to being re-schooled. The life of a Marine is one of study and change.

The basic Marine Expeditionary Unit (MEU) is a self-contained force. The typical MEU has fifteen hundred to three thousand Marines. These men and women are always prepared to board ships and go to any trouble spot in the world on short notice. MEUs have their own air arm, their own artillery, their own trucks and other support vehicles. The unit requires the services of radio operators, mechanics, cooks and bakers, as well as ground-pounding infantry. Special skills require special training. The Marine's job is to learn.

A Marine must always keep his or her "seabag" packed. A seabag is the tubular traveling "suitcase," or duffel bag, where Marines put all their gear. Marines are always on the move, and most members like it that way. The Marine Corps can be considered the nation's overseas police force. Wherever there is an emergency in the world, the call will sound—"send in the Marines." And of course the Marines will always respond.

Navy Hospital Corpsmen, Medics to the Marines

One job a Marine cannot hold is that of a medic. Marines do not directly tend to wounded on the battlefield. Navy medics, called Corpsmen, are assigned to the Marine Corps to provide first aid and assistance to the wounded and the sick. Over the years, the Corpsmen have become heroes to the Marines. Particularly in World War II, Corpsmen exposed themselves to enemy fire in order to treat Marines. Between 1914 and 1969, twenty-one Navy Medical Corpsmen have been awarded the Medal of Honor while serving with the Marines.

Marine Traditions

Falling into formation means just that. When your company is called upon to "fall in" on the company street, you are expected to be there bright and alert. If you work in an office, "falling in" means you must be at your desk at the exact time you are ordered to report.

Looking like a Marine is always important. A Marine stands straight, no slouching. Hat is properly on one's head. Hands are not in one's pockets. Many Marines refuse to smoke or chew gum in public because they believe such practices bring disgrace to their uniforms.

The Noncommissioned Officers

More than any other branch of service the Marine Corps relies on its noncommissioned officers, or NCOs, for leadership. An NCO is an enlisted leader and holds a status just below that of a commissioned officer (CO). All men and women, corporal and above, are NCOs. Upon becoming an NCO, he or she studies the Noncommissioned Officer's Creed:

> *I am the backbone of the United States Marine Corps, I am a Marine Noncommissioned Officer . . . I will demand of myself all the energy, knowledge, and skills I possess, so I can instill confidence in those I teach. I will constantly strive to perfect my own skills and to become a good leader.*[6]

It is a good idea to seek the advice and counsel of the senior men or senior women NCOs in your unit. Often this will be the gunnery sergeant or "Gunny." The gunnery sergeant is a concept unique to the Marines. The Gunny is a

No matter where they are, Marines have a duty to adhere to the principles of the Corps. This means wearing the uniform correctly, standing straight, and looking alert.

technical sergeant and is usually the highest-ranking enlisted person within a platoon of forty to sixty Marines. The gunnery sergeant is a sort of father figure for young Marines. The gunny can be a stern father. But leading a platoon is an enormous responsibility. Gunnies know the younger men and women yearn for fair guidance.

US Marines return from a live fire exercise in Australia. Marines are recognized by many as the toughest of all the armed forces. They have the most challenging path, and they're given the most dangerous assignments.

THE CHALLENGES AND REWARDS OF BEING A MARINE

We are mad, not only individually, but nationally. We check manslaughter and isolated murders; but what of war and the much vaunted crime of slaughtering whole peoples?

—Seneca, the Roman philosopher who died in 65 A.D. In his writings Seneca often criticized his nation's leaders who let passion overtake their reason and bring Rome to war.[1]

All the services recognize the Marines have some of the toughest standards of admission, the toughest training, and they are given the toughest assignments. President Ronald Reagan once said, "Some people spend an entire lifetime wondering if they made a difference. The Marines don't have that problem."[2]

Aside from the element of pride, service with the Marines is a job that offers pay and full benefits. The pay aspect is one few young Marines facing boot camp have time to think about. However, as a Marine, a man or woman is guaranteed food and lodging and complete health benefits. As long as duties are performed, there is no threat of layoffs. In times of an uncertain economy and a poor job market, military service beckons many high school grads. Do not expect to get rich. A beginning private entering boot camp has a military pay grade of E-1. This means the private earns $1,104 a month. Many civilian jobs open to high school grads pay three times that amount.

Marine pride stays with a person long after one's discharge. Marines who served together fifty or more years in the past get together to celebrate spirited reunions. The Marine experience is something a person will talk about, think about, and remember for a lifetime. In fact, many older veterans of the Corps refuse to say they are *ex*-Marines. They claim the prefix "ex" distances them from the USMC. "Once a Marine, always a Marine." So they call themselves "former" Marines rather than ex.

One former Marine was Ted Williams, who died in July 2002. In the 1940s and 1950s, Williams was one of the country's greatest baseball players. In his career, he hit 521 home runs. He was also a Marine officer and a pilot in World War II and in the Korean conflict. Williams maintained his experience as a Marine overshadowed his illustrious career as a ballplayer. He once said, "It's a funny thing, but as years go by, I think you appreciate more and more what a great thing it was to be a United States Marine. . . . I am a US Marine and I'll be one till I die."[3]

Marine Corps Careers

Most men and women will serve a three- or four-year obligation, or commitment, in the Corps and then return to civilian life. They will find their Marine training to be invaluable in the years ahead. Infantry training, which all Marines go through, gives a person discipline and a sense

Awards, Medals, and Decorations

On their dress uniforms, Marines proudly wear medals they were given for excellent performance of their duties. Here are some of the medals Marines are awarded, in order of precedence:

Medal of Honor—The highest award given by the American military, awarded for personal acts of valor above and beyond the call of duty.

Navy Cross—Given to Navy personnel and Marines for exceptional gallantry in combat.

Distinguished Service Medal—Presented only to officers who perform their duties with excellence.

Silver Star—Awarded for bravery beyond one's duty.

Bronze Star—Given for exceptional performance in military operations.

Purple Heart—Presented to those wounded or killed in combat.

Whether they remain in the Marine Corps or retire to civilian life, Marines always respect one another and share a deep bond.

of responsibility. Special skills such as mechanics or truck driving will apply directly to civilian jobs.

Many men and women will decide to forego civilian life and choose to remain in the Corps. Their ultimate goal is to establish a career and serve the Marines for twenty or more years before retiring. After twenty years as a Marine, a person will receive a generous pension and still be relatively young.

As their initial enlistment period expires, the Corps encourages its men and women to "ship over," or re-enlist. Certainly it benefits the Marine Corps to keep experienced men and women in its ranks. When one "ships over," he or she receives a substantial cash bonus. Reenlisting Marines usually sign up for three or six additional years. Often, upon shipping over, a Marine will get his or her choice of duty assignments.

Embassy duty is one of the most prestigious jobs in the Marine Corps. A Marine contingent stands guard at every American Embassy building in the world. Reenlistment is required to qualify for the special Embassy positions. Of course, even Embassy duty has its hazards. In November 1979 militant students stormed the American Embassy in Tehran, Iran, and held fifty-three Americans there captive. Among the hostages were thirteen Marines of the guard unit. The Marine guards had been ordered not to fire on the invading students. The Americans were held 444 days until their final release. One captive, muscular Marine Sergeant Rodney Sickman, frustrated his guards. Sickman challenged the Iranians to arm wrestling contests and beat them in every encounter.

Many interesting jobs and assignments are open to career Marines. More than 180 specialized skills are taught in

Some Famous Marines
Actors and TV Personalities

Drew Carey

Gene Hackman

Harvey Keitel

Lee Marvin

Ed McMahon

Steve McQueen

Burt Reynolds

Montel Williams

Athletes

Billy Mills (track star)

Ken Norton (boxer)

Leon Spinks Jr. (boxer)

Lee Trevino (golfer)

Ted Williams (baseball star)

Business and Political Leaders

James Baker (secretary of state)

F. Lee Bailey (lawyer)

John Glenn (US senator from Ohio
and astronaut)

John Murtha (US representative
from Pennsylvania)

James Webb (secretary of the Navy
and US senator from Virginia)

Fred Smith (founder of FedEx)

Amphibious assault vehicles depart the well deck of the dock ship.

Embassy duty is one of the most prestigious jobs in the Marines. Marine Guards are responsible for providing security at US embassies around the world.

Marine schools. Men and women learn electronics, weather forecasting, office management, construction, and dozens of other trades. But never forget, Marines are riflemen first. Anytime during the course of a career, one can expect a transfer to a combat unit.

Combat Duty

Making war is the ultimate task of the Marine Corps. All Marines prepare for war even though they hope they will never be called upon to fight. War is the most brutal, the most hurtful, the most dangerous activity engaged in by humankind. Yet warfare will touch the lives of many Marines.

Traditionally, the Leathernecks are given tough and dangerous combat assignments. Consequently, they experience a severe rate of casualties.

The Challenges and Rewards of Being a Marine

Terror prevails in every war. Combat veterans agree that a man who says he is not afraid in battle is either a liar or a fool. The fear in war is constant and mind-numbing. In Iraq and Afghanistan, there are no routine patrols or easy assignments. Combat wounds are particularly horrible. Wounds in Iraq include legs blown off due to land mine blasts and improvised explosive devices (IEDs). Other combat injuries result in agonizing burns, hideous facial scars or traumatic brain injury (TBI), similar to a concussion but more severe. Thanks to the prompt medical assistance available today, few of those injured die from their wounds. The survival rate among the wounded is far greater than in any previous war.

The stress of battle can leave scars beyond evident wounds to the body. The mind can endure only so much intense danger, only so many close brushes with death. Even after leaving a combat zone, memories of combat danger can torment a person's inner thoughts. Veterans of any war can suffer from what is called posttraumatic stress disorder (PTSD). This condition was called "shell shock" in World War I and "combat fatigue" in World War II. It is a mental disorder brought about by the stress of war. Nightmares, an inability to concentrate, irritability, and alarming flashbacks to scenes of combat haunt a victim of PTSD. Such mental demons can plague a person for years.

In 1880, the American Civil War General William T. Sherman spoke to an audience. To those youths in the audience who dreamed about finding glory in war, the general said, "There is many a boy here today who looks on war as all glory, but, boys it is all hell."[4]

Anyone wishing to join the Marines must weigh the risks against the rewards. The Marine experience can be

Books about and by Marines at War

With the Old Breed at Peleliu and Okinawa by Eugene Sledge, is one of the most powerful of all World War II memoirs. As a young Marine, Sledge saw intense combat in the Pacific. His book is not always complimentary to his fellow Marines. In painful detail, Sledge describes how war can transform otherwise respectable young men and turn them into cruel, unfeeling brutes.

Tom Brady went to Korea as a Marine Lieutenant in 1951. In his book *The Marines of Autumn*, he describes how he and his men faced two enemies: the bitter cold as well as the Chinese and North Korean Communists. Brady's book is a novel and an absorbing account of a winter campaign during the Korean War.

Former Virginia senator and secretary of the Navy, Jim Webb served in combat in Vietnam and wrote *Fields of Fire* shortly after returning home. It is a classic novel about three young men's journey into combat and jungle warfare of the Vietnam War.

Nathaniel Fick's *One Bullet Away: The Making of a Marine Officer* is a personal odyssey of a college classics major who wants an adventure and joins the Marines in 1999—just before the War on Terrorism begins. He artfully chronicles his combat tours in Iraq and Afghanistan and gives readers a close look at the frontlines and the contemporary Marine Corps.

Marines on the amphibious assault ship USS *Makin Island* climb into a Sea Knight helicoptor.

Marines are proud of their long and storied history. They know they are the best at what they do, but they also respect their brothers and sisters who have fallen at wartime.

immensely rewarding for a young person. However, it must be remembered that the ultimate task for a Marine is to wage war. And war, as General Sherman once said, is all hell.

The Future of the Marine Corps

On November 10, 2014, the Marine Corps celebrated its 239th birthday. The Commandant, General Dunford, issued his annual greeting to the Corps and noted that, in the previous twelve months, Marines had responded to crises in the Philippines, South Sudan, Libya, and Iraq— while still maintaining its decade-long combat operations in Afghanistan. As he said, "Some things change. This year found us in different climes and places than our predecessors in 1944 and 2004. We have adapted our organization, training, and equipment to the ever-changing operating environment. Some things remain the same. Marines attacked this year's challenges with the same courage, commitment, loyalty, self-sacrifice, and adaptability as their predecessors in Peleliu and Fallujah. For that reason, on 10 November 2014, we Marines can look back with pride on our accomplishments—confident in our ability to meet future challenges."[5]

APPENDIX: MILITARY SALARIES

Ranks and Salaries of Enlisted Men

Enlisted Rank	Pay Grade	Approximate Salary*	Insignia
Private	E-1	under 4 months: $1,430 per month; over 4 months: $1546.80 per month	No insignia
Private First Class	E-2	$1,734.00 per month	
Lance Corporal	E-3**	$1,823.40–2,055.30 per month	
Corporal	E-4	$2,019.60–2,451.60 per month	
Sergeant	E-5	$2,202.90–3,125.70 per month	
Staff Sergeant	E-6	$2,404.50–3,724.20 per month	
Gunnery Sergeant	E-7	$2,780.10–4,996.20 per month	
Master Sergeant	E-8	$3,999.00–5,703.60 per month	
First Sergeant	E-8	$3,999.00–5,703.60 per month	
Master Gunnery Sergeant	E-9	$4,885.20–7,584.60 per month	
Sergeant Major	E-9	$4,885.20–7,584.60 per month	
Sergeant Major of the Marine Corps	E-9	$4,885.20–7,584.60 per month	

* Approximate salaries are as of 2015 and do not include food and housing allowances, free healthcare, money for college, and bonuses.

** Salary for ranks E-3 through E-9 depend on the number of years in service.

Ranks and Salaries of Officers

Warrant Officers Rank	Pay Grade	Approximate Salary per month*	Insignia
Warrant Officer	W-1	$2,868.30–4,956.00	
Chief Warrant Officer	W-2	$3,267.30–5,453.70	
Chief Warrant Officer	W-3	$3,692.40–6,477.30	
Chief Warrant Officer	W-4	$4,043.40–7,531.80	
Chief Warrant Officer	W-5	$7,189.50–9,408.30	
Officers			
Second Lieutenant	O-1	$2,934.30–3,692.10	
First Lieutenant	O-2	$3,380.70–4,678.50	
Captain	O-3	$3,912.60–6,365.40	
Major	O-4	$4,449.90–7,430.10	
Lieutenant Colonel	O-5	$5,157.60–8,762.40	
Colonel	O-6	$6,186.60–10,952.40	
Brigadier General	O-7	$8,264.40–12,347.70	
Major General	O-8	$9,946.20–14,338.50	
Lieutenant General	O-9	$14,056.80-17,436.90	
General	O-10	$16,072.20–19,762.50	

* Approximate salaries are as of 2015 and do not include food and housing allowances, free healthcare, money for college, and bonuses.

** Salary for ranks E-3 through E-9 depend on the number of years in service.

NOVEMBER 10, 1775—The United States Marine Corps is created by an act of the Second Continental Congress; the official birthday of the Corps is still celebrated on November 10.

1776—During the American War of Independence, the US ship *Alfred* lands 268 Marines on the British-held island of New Providence in the Bahamas; it was the Marines first amphibious operation.

1805—The Marines attacked pirate bases at Derna, Tripoli.

1814—In a War of 1812 action, a unit of Marines and sailors put up a spirited defense against British troops near Washington, D.C.

1847—During the Mexican-American War the Marines conquered palace grounds once used by the Aztec leader Montezuma.

1859—Marines led by Army Colonel Robert E. Lee capture the antislavery zealot John Brown at Harpers Ferry, Virginia (now West Virginia); John Brown's raid at Harpers Ferry was a major cause of the Civil War (1861–1865).

1898—In the Spanish-American War the Marines were the first troops to land in Cuba and the first to land in the Philippines.

1912—Marines land at Nicaragua to put down a revolution in that nation; the Nicaragua operation was an example of the "little war" the Marines have been called upon to fight throughout their history.

1917—Marines are transported to France to take part in World War I.

Timeline

1918—The Marines fight the biggest battle thus far in their history at Belleau Wood in France.

1918—The first women join the Marines Corps; the first Marine airwing is established.

1926—The Marines again land at Nicaragua.

1941—The Japanese bomb Pearl Harbor on December 7, plunging the United States into World War II.

1942—Marines land at Guadalcanal to begin the US World War II offensive in the Pacific.

1943—The four-day battle of Tarawa Atoll cost the Marines more than one thousand lives.

1944—Marines assault Peleliu, a dismal Pacific Island, and begin a bloody battle that lasts more than five weeks.

1945—In a terrible battle the Marines conquer Iwo Jima from Japanese defenders.

1945—Marines participate in the Battle of Okinawa, the costliest single battle in the Pacific War.

1945—World War II ends with Marine casualties listed as 19,733 killed and 67,204 wounded in almost four years of warfare.

1950—North Korea invades South Korea, thereby launching the Korean War.

1950–51—During a bitter winter campaign, surrounded Marines fight out of the Chosen Reservoir in Korea.

1953—The Korean War ends; the Marines have suffered 28,011 casualties in three years of fighting.

1962—Marine officer and pilot John Glenn becomes the first American to orbit the earth when his spacecraft, *Friendship 7*, blasted into the sky and circled the earth three times on February 20.

1965—Marines begin operations in Vietnam; they are the first regular troops the United States deployed in that country.

1968—In an assault on the Vietnamese city of Hue, the Marines suffer one thousand men killed or wounded.

1973—The Vietnam War ends; almost eight hundred thousand Marines have served in Vietnam over the years and more than thirteen thousand were killed during the fighting.

1983—A bomb planted by a suicide bomber kills 220 Marines in Lebanon.

1991—Marines take part in the Persian Gulf War.

1992—Marines serve as peacekeepers and help quell a civil war in the African nation of Somalia.

1997—Marines return to Africa and help feed starving people in the war-torn nation of Sierra Leone.

2001—Marines are the first regular troops employed in Afghanistan after the September 11 terrorist attacks.

2003—Marines are key participants in the Iraq War.

2004—Marines participate in humanitarian operations in various Asian countries after the December tsunami tidal wave took many thousands of lives and left millions homeless.

2004—Marines fight the First and Second Battles of Fallujah against insurgents in Iraq, resulting in some of the heaviest urban combat US Marines have been involved in since the battle at Hue in Vietnam.

2010—The Secretary of Defense repeals the ban on homosexuals in the military, allowing gays to openly serve in all services.

2011—The United States completes the withdrawal of troops from Iraq.

2013—The Secretary of Defense repeals the restrictions on women in combat, opening up thousands of positions in the military.

CHAPTER NOTES

CHAPTER 1   First In!

1. Elena Schneider, NYTimes.com, June 19, 2014.
2. http://www.cmohs.org/recipient-detail/3511/carpenter-william-kyle.php.
3. Elena Schneider, NYTimes.com, June 19, 2014.

CHAPTER 2   The Few, the Proud

1. B.L. Crumley, *The Marine Corps* (San Diego, Calif.: Thunder Bay Press, 2002), p. 9.
2. Scott Keller, *Marine Pride* (New York: Kensington Publishers, 2004), p. 117.
3. Joseph H. Alexander, *The Battle History of the US Marines* (New York: Harper Collins, 1999), p. 47.

CHAPTER 3   The Second World War

1. George Feifer, *The Battle of Okinawa* (Guilderford, Conn.: Globe Press, 2001), p. 258.
2. Rafael Steinberg, *Island Fighting* (Alexandria, Va.: Time-Life Book, 1978), pp. 112–113.
3. Ibid., p. 118.
4. Ibid.
5. E.B. Sledge, *With the Old Breed on Peleliu and Okinawa* (New York: Oxford University Press, 1981), p. 125.
6. Scott Keller, *Marine Pride* (New York: Kensington Publishers, 2004), p. 136.
7. Joseph H. Alexander, *The Battle History of the US Marines* (New York: Harper Collins, 1999), p. 248.

CHAPTER 4   The Corps and the Changing World

1. Joseph H. Alexander, *The Battle History of the US Marines* (New York: Harper Collins, 1999), p. 352.

2. Ibid., p. 270.

3. Ibid., p. 291.

4. Harry G. Summers, *Korean War Almanac* (New York: Facts on File, 1990), p. 75.

5. Alexander, p. 360.

6. Ibid., p. 340.

7. Scott Keller, *Marine Pride* (New York: Kensington Publishers, 2004), p. 151.

8. Edwin Howard Simmons, ed., *The Marines* (Quantico, Va.: Marine Corps Heritage Foundation, 1998), p. 105.

9. Alexander, p. 376.

10. Rubin, Alissa. "Comrades Speak of Fallen Marine and Ties That Bind," *New York Times*, February 1, 2008.

11. http://www.defense.gov/news/casualty.pdf.

12. The Associated Press, "Marines Hit the Ravaged Beaches," *The Orange County Register*, January 11, 2005, <http://www.ocregister.com/ocr/2005/01/11/. sections/nation_world/asia_pacificrim/Article_373053.php> (August 25, 2006).

CHAPTER 5   The Marine Corps Today

1. S.F. Tomajczyk, *To Be a US Marine* (St. Paul, Minn.: Zenith Press, 2004), p. 135.

2. Edwin Howard Simmons, ed., *The Marines* (Quantico, Va.: Marine Corps Heritage Foundation, 1998), p. 241.

CHAPTER 6   So You Want to Be a Marine?

1. S.F. Tomajczyk, *To Be a US Marine* (St. Paul, Minn.: Zenith Press, 2004), p. 47.

2. Ibid., p. 64.

3. Ibid.

Chapter Notes

CHAPTER 7   Marine Training

1. http://www.hqmc.marines.mil/Portals/142/Docs/36th%20 CMC's%20Message%20for%20all%20Marines.pdf.
2. *Concepts and Programs* 2005 (an official US Marine publication), p. 65.

CHAPTER 8   The Marine Corps Family

1. Joseph H. Alexander, *The Battle History of the US Marines* (New York: Harper Collins, 1999), p. xi.
2. Ibid., p. 248.
3. http://www.womensmemorial.org/PDFs/StatsonWIM.pdf.
4. Edwin Howard Simmons, ed., *The Marines* (Quantico, Va.: Marine Corps Heritage Foundation, 1998), p. 71.
5. *Concepts and Programs* 2015 (an official US Marine publication.
6. S.F. Tomajczyk, *To Be a US Marine* (St. Paul, Minn.: Zenith Press, 2004), p. 54.

CHAPTER 9   The Challenges and Rewards of Being a Marine

1. Bergen Evens, ed., *Dictionary of Quotations* (New York: Wings Books, 1993), p. 736.
2. S. F. Tomajczyk, *To Be a US Marine* (St. Paul, Minn.: Zenith Press, 2004), p. 135.
3. Scott Keller, *Marine Pride* (New York: Kensington Publishers, 2004), opening page.
4. Evens, p. 734.
5. http://www.hqmc.marines.mil/Portals/142/Docs/USMC%20 239TH%20BIRTHDAY%20MESSAGE%20FROM%20 CMC(FINAL).pdf.

US Marines conduct a beach landing training exercise on Green Beach at Camp Pendleton, California.

anonymous—An unnamed person, usually a writer.

boot camp—Marine basic training (usually a three-month course) given to all Marine enlisted men and women.

carnage—Excessive gore or pain.

chaotic—Extremely confusing.

commandant—The top-ranked Marine, usually a four-star general.

contingent—A small military unit.

dedicate—To present a monument or a statue in a public ceremony.

elite—Superior, better than the others.

escalate—To increase or grow greater; the term was often used to describe how the Vietnam War expanded year-by-year.

ethnic groups—Groups of people based on their nationalities.

fixed-wing aircraft—Any airplane with a fixed or standard wing; helicopters having rotating wings are not fixed-wing craft.

memoir—A written account of an experience.

mutiny—The act of forcibly taking over a ship.

OCS (Officer Candidate School)—Boot camp for officers; the officers basic training course.

posttraumatic stress disorder (PTSD)—Symptoms that may develop after a person is exposed to one or more traumatic events. The diagnosis may be given when a group of symptoms, such as disturbing flashbacks, avoidance or numbing of memories of the traumatic event, and hyperarousal, continue for more than a month after the traumatic event.

prefix—A syllable in front of a word that alters that word.

reluctantly—To act slowly, without commitment.

repress—To quell or restrain.

robotic—Machine-driven aircraft or ground vehicles.

seabag—Marine Corps-issued duffel bag.

ship over—Marine slang for reenlisting.

symbolize—To represent an object with another object, as a flag represents a nation.

tsunami—The massive tidal wave that swept over Pacific countries in 2004; the Marines assisted thousands of tsunami victims.

Vietcong—Vietnamese resistance fighters who fought Americans in the Vietnam War.

zealot—A person pursuing a cause with excessive enthusiasm.

FURTHER READING

Books

Blair, Jane. *Hesitation Kills: A Female Marine Officer's Combat Experience in Iraq*. Lanham, Md.: Rowman & Littlefield Publishers, 2011.

Campbell, Donovan. *Joker One: A Marine Platoon's Story of Courage, Leadership, and Brotherhood*. New York: Random House Paperback, 2010.

Dowling, Mike. *Sergeant Rex: The Unbreakable Bond Between a Marine and His Military Working Dog*. New York: Atria, 2012.

Klay, Phil. *Redeployment*. New York: Penguin Books, 2014.

Shulimson, Jack, Major Charles M. Johnson, and the US Marine Corps History and Museums Division. *US Marines in Vietnam: The Landing and the Buildup—1965 (Marine Corps Vietnam Series)*. Seattle: Amazon Publishing, 2013.

US Marine Corps and Charles Smith. *US Marines in the Korean War*. Seattle: Amazon Publishing, 2014.

West, Bing. *One Million Steps: A Marine Platoon At War*. New York: Random House, 2014.

Web Sites

usmcmuseum.com/index.asp

The National Museum of the Marine Corps' official Web site has virtual tours of the galleries, recordings, 3-D aircraft models, and more.

usmc.mil/

Learn about the units, view photos, and read the latest news at the official site of the US Marine Corps.

marines.com/

Visit the United States Marine Corps Recruiting Web site for information about enlisting.

Movies

Flags of Our Fathers. Directed by Clint Eastwood. Hollywood, Calif.: Paramount Pictures, 2006.
Dramatizes the Battle of Iwo Jima.

Full Metal Jacket. Directed by Stanley Kubrick. Burbank, Calif.: Warner Bros., 1987.
Follows Marines from boot camp to the Vietnam War.

INDEX

Index

combat duty, 106–107, 111
future of, 111
medals and awards, 101
minorities in, 91–92, 94
nicknames, 19, 21, 55
qualifications for, 42, 62–64
talk, 11, 64–65
training, 23, 42, 54, 58, 66–69,
71–79, 81–86, 95, 99–101,
111
Marine Corps War Memorial, 32
"Marine Hymn," 12, 14, 69
Marine Reserves, 54–55, 57
Mexican-American War, 14
military draft, 63
Mills, Billy, 92, 94, 104
Montezuma, 14
Military Operations Other Than
War (MOOTWS), 48–49
M16 rifle, 65, 67, 75–76
MV-22 Osprey, 83–84
Myatt, Mike, 42

N

Navajo Code Talkers, 28, 30
Naval Academy, 33, 71, 89
New Providence Island, 12
Nicaragua, 16
Nicholas, Samuel, 57
Nimitz, Chester, 32
noncommissioned officers
(NCOs), 72, 96–97

O

O'Bannon, Presley N., 12
Obama, Barack 6, 47
Officer Candidate School (OCS),
72

Okinawa, 24, 28, 32–33, 53, 89,
108

P

Panama, 16
Panetta, Leon, 89
Parris Island, 66, 74, 89
Pearl Harbor, 22
Peleliu, Battle of, 24, 25, 27–28,
111
Pentagon, 44
Persian Gulf War, 42, 44
Petersen, Frank E., 91
Petraeus, David, 46
Philippines, 16–17, 111
pirates, 12
posttraumatic stress disorder
(PTSD), 107
Puerto Rico, 16
Pusan Perimeter, 36

Q

Quantico, Virginia, 72, 89
Quijada, Juan, 49

R

racial minorities, 88, 92
Reagan, Ronald, 99–100
Red Dogs, 55
Reynolds, Loretta, 89
robotic aircraft, 84
Roosevelt, Franklin, 27–28
Rosenthal, Joe, 30, 32
Rupertus, William, 62
Russia. *See* Soviet Union.

S

Saipan, 24
San Diego, California, 66–68, 74